# HARTLEYS

## Brick by Brick - Pot by Pot

### DAVID WILDERS

*Best Wishes*
*David Wilders*

Castleford
Press

**2003**

**Publisher**:     Castleford Press
                   8 West View Avenue, Redhill, Castleford,
                   West Yorkshire, WF10 3AQ

© Text:            David Wilders

Editors:           Brian Lewis and Lorna Hey
Cover Design       Harry Malkin

Printer:           FM Repro Ltd, Roberttown, Liversedge, West Yorkshire WF15 7NB

ISBN               0-9543689-0-8

This book has been five years in the making. Researching and recording has been a most interesting and fascinating way to pass time. Along the way I have had the privilege of meeting many interesting people, all have been enthusiastic and eager to help. I would like to thank them all for allowing me to interview them and for being there when ever I needed more information. When giving an insight in to the working of a local pottery and brickworks, workers' memories have brought a personal feel to local history. I owe a debt of gratitude to: Audrey Limbert, Wyn Winstanley, Pat Bentley, June Riley, John Brough, June Bott, Wilf Beedle, Norma Skeates, Terry Gill, Joan Brough, Ray Skeates, Doreen Hartley, Derrick Hopton, Mary Hopton, Arthur Green, George Jackson, Jean Wilkinson, Everett Hartley, Geoff Cheesbrough and Bill Oxberry.

I am gratful to all collectors for allowing me to access, photograph and catalogue their Hartrox collection, of which some are used in the book. I would also like to thank the following for the use of their photographs: Tableware International, Wakefield Libraries and Information Services, David Wilson and Ron Rockett. Also Normanton Brick Works for allowing me to take photographs of their works, and Castleford Library, Pontefract Library, John Goodchild, Ordnance Survey and the Pontefract and Castleford Express for access to their research material.

# CONTENTS

*This book is dedicated
to my wife Julie,
and daughter Leanne.*

# INTRODUCTION

A year after I was born, forty two-years ago, the last surviving pottery in Castleford, Clokie & Co. closed. So, like myself there is a generation of local people who have grown up unaware that Castleford once had a thriving pottery industry. It wasn't until researching for an earlier book, *History of Castleford,* that I discovered the significant role the pottery industry contributed, historically and economically to the development and evolution of Castleford.

Being inquisitive I wanted to know more. Armed with the knowledge that pieces of Castleford Pottery could still be purchased I went in search of a piece. At a local antique 'fare' I purchased my first piece, a small hand decorated stoneware bowl, marked *'Hartrox'.* The dealer was rather vague about the background history of the manufacturer. However, he assured me it was made in Castleford by Hartleys.

With my newly acquired piece of pottery in hand, I found myself asking, where, when, who and how was this item made? Coincidentally,  just after my purchase an antique shop opened in town. I introduced myself to the owner and informed her of my research plans and asked if she could pass on to me any names of persons whom she came in contact with through the shop. I wanted to meet people who had worked for Hartleys. She did. That is where my research really began.

My first contact was a Mrs Wyn Winstanley. Wyn had worked at the pottery, hand-decorating the wares. Eager and enthusiastic, with her help, I contacted other ex- employees, and we organised a reunion. This proved fruitful; we had more names.

At Hartleys the production of bricks and pottery went hand in hand. At some points the brick side of the business was in the ascendancy; at others the pottery. For this reason I have showed the importance of this duel economy in the sections *Brick by Brick* and *Pot by Pot.* This book is not a definitive account of the works, it is only a small token account. There is lots of scope for additional information. However by interviewing and recording the workers of the long established and respected Castleford family of Hartley, getting recollections of their work and life at the pottery and brickworks my knowledge increased. Their contributions are denoted in italicised text. This has enabled me to document a bygone era, and in that way add a small piece to the larger jigsaw, the Castleford pottery industry.

Although this book concentrates and documents one particular manufacturer it is necessary to give a broader view of Castleford's geology and the early history. In that way acknowledgement of the development of pottery and brick manufacturing at Hartleys is placed in the context.

A brick is a brick, a cup is a cup, but few ever stop to think where these essential everyday common objects are made or where the materials used to make them come from. The answer for a long time for many pieces was right here in Castleford.

From the early eighteenth century to the middle of the twentieth century Castleford was renowned as a world wide thriving commercial centre in the manufacturing of quality pottery and bricks. During this period several potteries and brickworks were established at various sites around the town. However, the most concentrated area was in Whitwood Mere, an area west of central Castleford. Here the abundance of natural clay, that in some places lay only a few feet from the surface, was easily accessible.

The many different wares that the Castleford potteries produced are today very scarce and collectable. They command high prices, being prized and collected by local people and museums, yet there is little visual evidence left in Whitwood Mere to link this important site to its industrial and manufacturing past. There are a few rows of workers terrace houses left, some old pottery buildings such as Clokie's look on to the River Calder and some surviving street names such as Pottery Street, and Phillips Street. That area of Whitwood Mere is still commonly referred to as the Potteries.

The prosperity and development of the pottery and other industries are directly attributed to Castleford's geographical location. Industry made the place and at its root lay coal, sand, clay and limestone, all locked in the underground strata beneath our feet. It was these deposits that beckoned the later industrialists who extracted, excavated, quarried and mined in to the bowels of this once sleepy agricultural village. They transformed it into a thriving commercial town.

Castleford is in the West Riding of Yorkshire. The town is situated in the eastern fringe of the lower Aire valley which overlays the Leeds and Nottingham coal field. The popular geological term given to the coal fields is *coal measures*. These coal measures were formed millions of years ago during the Carboniferous Period. The rich black coal seams provided work and prosperity to the town for over a hundred years. Coal was mined until the mid 1980s by the collieries of Fryston, Wheldale, Glasshoughton and Allerton Bywater. Coal heated the worker's homes and fuelled the factories, potteries, brick ovens and the glass furnaces. Closely associated with the formation of the coal measures are also seams of shales, mud stones and fireclay. These primary clays lay under most of Castleford and were utilised in the making of pottery, bricks and products allied to the building trade.

Secondary clays were deposited because of the River Aire. To the west of Castleford, some forty miles away on the high grounds of the Pennines and the Yorkshire Dales, the rivers Calder and Aire begin life. They descend until they finally join and become one at Castleford. Where these two rivers converge the intense amount of water has caused a massive overspill, and mass flooding to the surrounding low lying area. On the flood plains were deposited the suspended particles of fine grains of sands and silts that derive from the upper regions through erosion. These deposits are called alluvium. The over-spill spanned a large area from Methley Bridge to the west of Castleford, down through Whitwood Mere along Aire Street and eastwards to Wheldale and Fryston and then northwards as far as Methley Mires, Allerton Bywater, Newton and the Fairburn Ings. It is these alluvium deposits of clay which were initially excavated and utilised in the early manufacturing of local pottery and brick, for it was easy to access. In some areas it lay only a few feet from the surface. It was to the sides of the River Aire that the new industries anchored themselves utilising it as a source of power and transportation as it flowed through the town eastwards to meet the River Ouse, the Humber and then flowed on to the port of Hull.

The manufacturing of pottery is an ancient practice. Pottery had been made in England 5500 years ago. Archaeologists use pottery as a tool to date sites and artefacts. When looking back to find links with Castleford's past, there is an interesting possibility that pottery was being made in our local region from 3400 years ago. Three miles to the east of central Castleford in an area once covered in woodlands, was a site for Bronze Age burials. The burial mounds were excavated in the nineteenth century by W. Greenwell in what is now the Parish of Ferrybridge. The burial grounds situated near Straglands Lane are now covered by

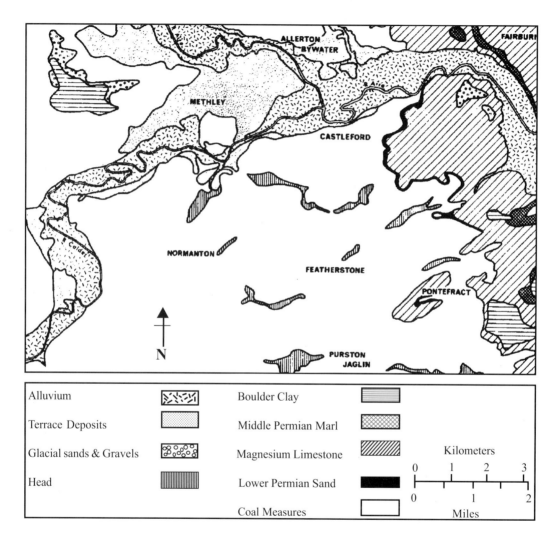

| Alluvium | | Boulder Clay | |
| Terrace Deposits | | Middle Permian Marl | |
| Glacial sands & Gravels | | Magnesium Limestone | |
| Head | | Lower Permian Sand | |
| | | Coal Measures | |

Kilometers

0   1   2   3

0   1   2

Miles

A Simplified Geological Map.

a golf course and Ferrybridge Power Station. These were also excavated much later in the early 1960s. These graves produced rich pottery finds, a beaker, collared urns and a food vessel. The finds are at present housed at The British Museum in London, and are subject to further study. Although these finds are believed by the professionals to be imported in to the area, it cannot be ruled out that there were inhabited enclosures in this area, and that the people used the natural deposits of alluvial clay from the banks of the nearby River Aire for basic cooking and storing vessels.

Some two thousand years later Castleford was inhabited by the Romans. Their occupation has been recognised by passing antiquarians such as William Camden in 1586 and William Stukeley in 1724, for Lagentium was an important site having both a Roman fort and settlement. This knowledge has been extended as more and more Roman artefacts have been found, and the Roman fort unearthed by modern methods of archaeology.

The Romans fortified an encampment close to the south bank of the River Aire from late first century. They brought with them their building expertise. They had manufacturing skills to sustain a fort and vicus, the civilian settlement that evolved around the military settlement. We know from the archaeologists' finds that the Romans imported large amounts of quality Samian Ware pottery, a smooth red glossy high quality table ware manufactured in Gaul, as well as utilitarian wares from Spain and Germany. Nearer to home potters in Dorset, Colchester, Lincolnshire, and Doncaster also sent their wares to Castleford.

There is also evidence that the Romans set up commercial potteries in Yorkshire near Doncaster, Malton and North Humberside. Their primary consideration in the positioning of a pottery was the availability of a good source of clay, sand, water, fuel and in close proximity to local markets and forts. These requirements fit Castleford quite well and the Romans utilised the surrounding area's raw materials to produce pottery. Recently experts have analysed the fabric of the finds excavated from the digs at Castleford. A large proportion of coarseware pottery sherds found have an unknown origin, but some are of local origin.

Several pottery sherds have been typed as Castleford Grey Ware, so manufactured in Castleford. We also have fragments of mortaria, shallow dishes used for grinding herbs and spice. These are likely to have been from a local workshop. Further excavations revealed nearly 1000 fragments of clay moulds used to make enamelled vessels. Also, over 800 fragments of clay moulds found were used for casting spoons with purse-shaped bowls. They are dated from the later Castleford Roman period, that is from the third and fourth centuries of the Modern Era. On analysis the fabric of the spoon moulds was found to be made from fireclay probably obtained in the Castleford area. To date there has been no evidence found of Roman kilns in Castleford, but time and future excavations will possibly reveal some.

Bricks as a building material were popularised in Britain by the Romans. From the fort at Castleford, two half round bricks were recovered. They were produced from local material and some were probably used for ornamental purposes or to make up circular columns. Parts of roof tiles were also unearthed at three different locations, the fort, bathhouse and vicus. Again experts suggest a local source of clay.

The replacement of the urban/fort economy with the villa/hamlet one in the fifth and sixth centuries resulted in the shift of the local population, ending of extensive urbanisation, and the consequent demise of the local brick and pottery industry. There is little evidence that Castleford was inhabited in the fifth century and there is very little recorded information of life in Castleford up to the tenth century.

Although pottery has been made in Yorkshire since the earliest times, it was in the Medieval Period that new techniques and the art of making pots developed. This manufacture did not affect Castleford though it did affect the growth of other local settlements. In the early sixteenth century a local pottery industry was established at Wrenthorpe, known then as Potovens near Outwood. However, it was much later in the early eighteenth century that the brick and pottery industry, be it on a small scale, began at Castleford. By the mid- nineteenth century Castleford had ten working potteries and a further three in Ferrybridge. Since the Yorkshire region production peaked in this period with over 100 potteries producing wares, this amounts to 13% of the region's potteries, Castleford was competing with Leeds, the only centre to outstrip it in this period.

The use of brick as a building material in our region was not common until the late seventeenth century. One of the earliest local brick buildings in the Wakefield area is the substantial house Clarke Hall, near Stanley, which was built in the 1670s. At this time most domestic buildings continued to be timber framed with the more important buildings built of local stone. By the early eighteenth century brick making was taking place in the Wakefield area, be it on a small domestic scale, where kilns supplied the developing towns of Pontefract and Wakefield. These fashionable towns were beginning to use bricks for domestic housing and public buildings.

Brick making had become most popular in the parts of the county that were deficient in building stone, and also in areas with a dense population, where bricks had become a cheaper alternative. These areas were chiefly associated with the fast growing industrial communities which grew around the many coalfields. Many local collieries such as Prince of Wales, Glasshoughton, Fryston, Ackton Hall, St. John's and Briggs produced their own bricks, utilising the bands of clay and shale found within the coal seams for the construction of miner's cottages, colliery buildings and underground consumption. As time passed colliery manufacture diminished and the local brick yards made it uneconomical for the mines to carry on manufacturing.

During the mid to late nineteenth century the brick industry in Castleford was booming. The key factors being the demand for bricks which led to the introduction of new efficient manufacturing methods. The development of new brick making machines replaced the laborious work of hand-moulding. The other major improvement area was in the type of kiln used. The widely used Scotch-type kiln which was an open top structure in which the bricks were stacked upon each other in their thousands, loosely covered with burnt bricks and fired in one go, was superseded by the introduction of a Continuous Kiln. The innovator who brought about these changes was a local inventor, John Craven from Wakefield, whose background was in engineering, designed the revolutionary stiff plastic process brick making machinery. This process pressed and moulded hard clays and shales to produce a dense brick which required little drying. He subsequently started his own brickworks on Dewsbury Road, Wakefield and in 1862 installed the first Hoffman Continuous Kiln in England. The Hoffmann Continuous Kiln was developed in Germany in about 1858. The early kilns of this type took the form of great circular ring chambers with massive walls and a chimney at the centre. The kiln had twelve brick-burning chambers which were filled with bricks which dried, baked and cooled before the chambers were emptied in turn. The new continuous types of kilns required a lower fuel consumption and incurred less heat loss, this shifted the production economy of small outputs into a huge factory phase. This type of kiln, later increased in length to accommodate more burning chambers, changed in shape to an elliptical form. Rectangular forms were also in use in the various brickworks of Castleford.

Brick manufacturing was becoming a big business and a profitable one. This attracted other local entrepreneurs and influential businessmen such as James Phillips, an architect, surveyor and valuer. He ran the North Eastern Steam Brick and Pipe Works in the 1850s. The glass magnates also turned their hands to brick making. James Winterbottom, who in 1853 was a leading glass manufacturer, made tiles, fire bricks and sanitary pipes at the West Riding Bottle and Brick Works. So did Edger Breffit, owner of the Aire and Calder Bottle Works, and Sykes and Macvay of the Albion Glass Bottle Works. The Potters John and Thomas Clegg of The Mount Pleasant Pottery, Whitwood Mere, manufactured blue printed and white earthen ware from 1853, later they are recorded as maltsters, but they were also listed as brick makers in 1888.

The history of the many pottery works in Castleford is extensive in itself and complicated for many of the potteries were owned by the same people, company or companies who moved from one site to another. In the Appendix a list gives a snap shot through the early nineteenth century to the mid twentieth century of some of the potteries and brickworks that operated in Castleford.

By the late 1940s, Castleford had just three working brick manufacturers and three potteries. The gradual overall decline of the old industries saw Castleford's last producing pottery at Clokie & Company. This pottery closed in 1961 and Castleford saw the end of brick making when The Yorkshire Brick Company in Glasshoughton closed in 1977.

# Brick by Brick

# HARTLEYS THE PIONEERS

Joshua Hartley, (c.1820-1877) the founder of Hartleys (Castleford) Limited was born at Newton Lane End, Stanley. His father, William Hartley, was a brick maker of Wakefield. Nineteen years later Joshua was living in Dewsbury where in October 1839 he married Mary Ibbotson. Eventually Joshua and Mary had nine children: Charlotte, William, Sarah, Anne, Everett, Charles Ibbotson, Joshua, Arthur, and George Thomas. The first two of their children were born at Westgate Common, near Wakefield, and the third child at Daw Green, Crigglestone. The family moved to Whitwood Mere in 1850. The 1851 Census records him and his family living at Pottery Lane, later called Pottery Street.

By the mid century Joshua had started up his own business as a chimney-pot maker, employing two men, two boys and one girl. Sometime later he went in to partnership with George Turner Taylor, working from the Castleford Pottery of Garrett & Fletcher's, a property which they leased for £100 a year. The pottery, which had been established in the early part of the 1800s, was situated between Eastfield Lane and Healdfield Road on a site now between Gladstone Terrace and the Territorial and Volunteer Reserves Headquarters. Originally trading as Taylor and Hartley they quickly changed the pottery name to the Castleford Clay Works and produced blackware and stoneware pottery, firebricks and sanitary pipes. In 1852 Isaac Fletcher, the works owner, died. His family had to re-mortgage the pottery and this possibly led the partnership Taylor and Hartley to move on. Sometime in the mid 1850s they had acquired land and opened the Victoria Clay Works on a site south of Methley Road, Whitwood Mere, adjacent to the Russell's Pottery that backed on to the North Eastern Railway line. The entrance to the works was at the bottom of Wellington Street.

The times ahead were prosperous ones for the company for the country was experiencing an industrial boom. Industrial development was bringing large numbers of workers to townships. This in turn created the need for worker's houses. Castleford itself was also growing rapidly and migrant workers were flooding in to man the expanding glass, pottery, brick, chemical and labour intensive industries. Population figures show us that in 1811 the population of Castleford was 890, by 1831 it had risen to 1,141 and in 1851 it was 2,150. An

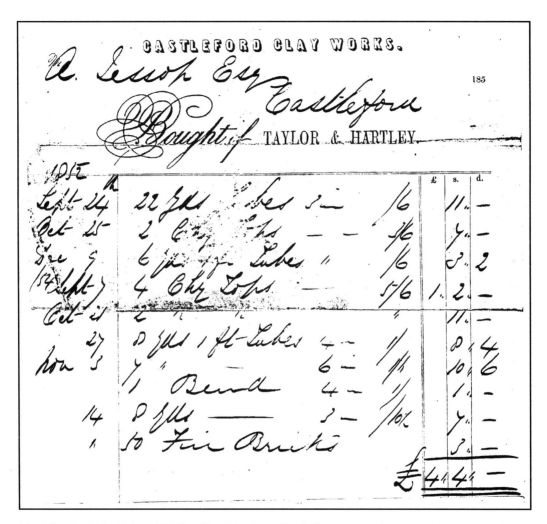

A Castleford Clay Works bill dated 1852. The bill is to Adam Jessop Esq. for four pounds and four shillings for the purchase of tubes, chimney tops, bends and fire bricks.

increase of 125% in forty years. By 1901 when Castleford was surrounded by coal mines the population of the town had risen to 17,386. Add this figure to the surrounding townships of Allerton Bywater, Whitwood and Glasshoughton, the population of the area to the north of Pontefract was 28,725, in fact not substantially smaller than today.

To cope with a growing community in 1851 a Local Board of Health was established to govern the town. This elementary local government implemented social changes. New houses, paved streets, drainage, water and gas works, along with public buildings, schools, shops churches, banks, businesses and industrial factories appeared. This development ensured that the brickworks produced a vast amount of red bricks. To meet this demand the Victoria Clay Works manufactured a variety of items all allied to the building trade such as sanitary tubes, chimney tops, fire bricks, quarries, red bricks, pan tiles, drain tiles and ridge tiles.

Castleford was ideally situated, since 1840 the town was linked to the railway network, and the navigable Aire and Calder river and canal system was ideal for carrying heavy bulky materials. The Victoria Clay Works had a wharf and a rail-siding. Although the railway system offered a speedy delivery it was at a higher cost. However, both were used, this ensured bricks and other wares were easily transported to other large and expanding towns. It is worth noting that the expanding railways themselves consumed enormous numbers of bricks in the building of bridges and tunnels.

The business prospered and so did Joshua. In the mid 1860s he had moved his home to Stottfield House, in Lumley Street, Hightown. In 1869 his business partner George Turner Taylor died but Joshua Hartley kept the business going and was trading in 1874 as Joshua Hartley and Company (late Taylor & Hartley). At least three of Joshua's sons, Everett, Charles and Joshua had interest in the family business. Everett Hartley was apprenticed to his father at Victoria Clay Works where he learned engineering and clay working. He was probably encouraged by his father to branch away from the family business. At the age of twenty-four, in 1876, he became manager of a similar type of business at Ardsley, near Wakefield, then in 1878 he acquired an interest in Monkhill Sanitary Pipe and Brickworks, Pontefract. In the proceeding years he managed the Woodman Sanitary Pipe and Brickworks in Elland and later he became the managing director of the Star Brick and Tile Company Limited in Monmouthshire. Everett died in Newport in 1919. His son Arthur Everett Hartley,

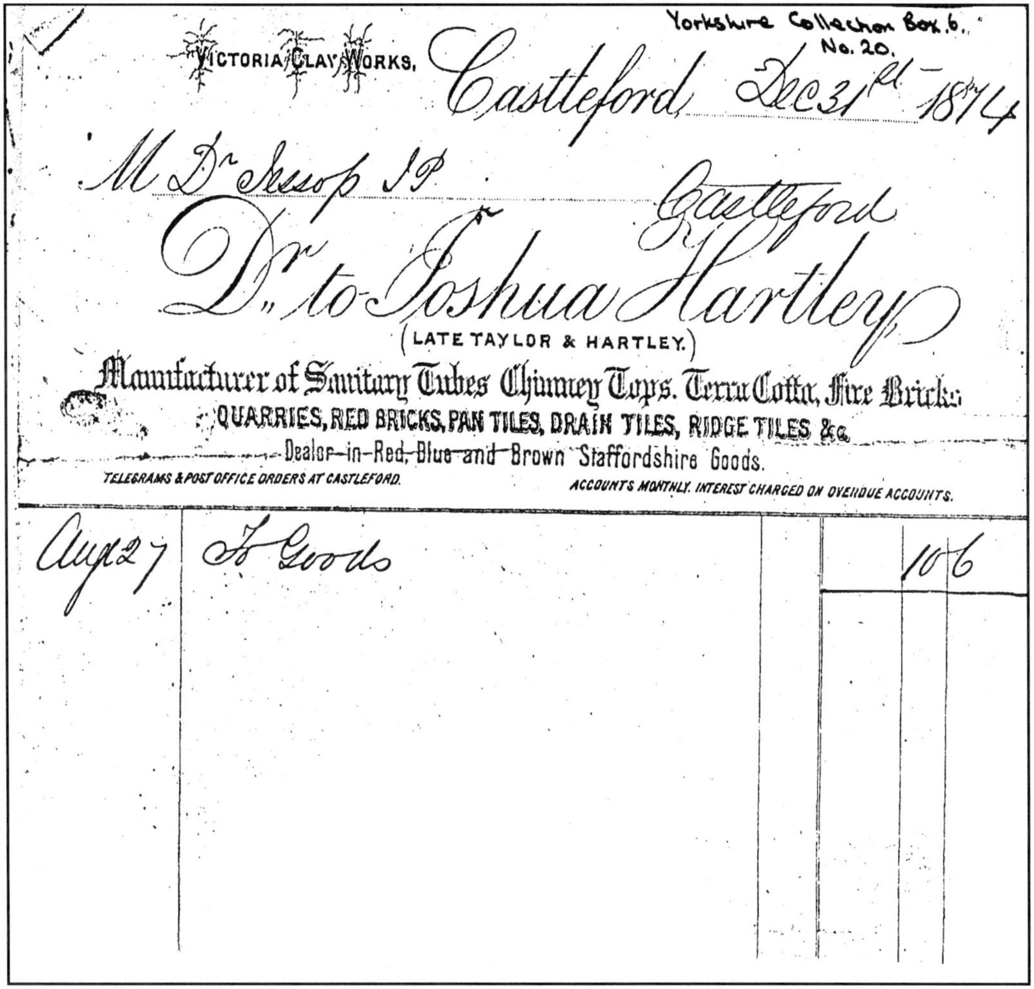

*Yorkshire Collection Box.6.*
*No. 20.*

VICTORIA CLAY WORKS,

*Castleford, Dec 31st 1874*

*M Dr Jessop JP                    Castleford*

*Dr to Joshua Hartley*

(LATE TAYLOR & HARTLEY.)

Manufacturer of Sanitary Tubes Chimney Tops. Terra Cotta, Fire Bricks.

QUARRIES, RED BRICKS, PAN TILES, DRAIN TILES, RIDGE TILES &c.

Dealer-in-Red, Blue and Brown Staffordshire Goods.

TELEGRAMS & POST OFFICE ORDERS AT CASTLEFORD.          ACCOUNTS MONTHLY. INTEREST CHARGED ON OVERDUE ACCOUNTS.

| Aug 27 | To Goods | | 10 6 |

This Victoria Clay Works bill shows the range of goods manufactured.

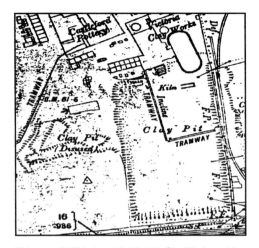

This map of 1898 shows the Victoria Clay Works and the adjacent Phillips Pottery, named here as Castleford Pottery, both having tramways in to the clay pit.

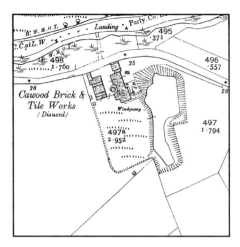

The Cawood Brick & Tile Works in 1908 is shown as disused. Joshua Hartley & Co. purchased the works in 1906 and resumed the production of bricks and tiles.

a solicitor, bought in to a practice in Castleford in 1911. The legal practice sited in Bank Street is now Hartley and Worstenholme.

Joshua senior died in 1877, and was succeeded by his two sons, Charles and Joshua Hartley. In 1888, Charles Hartley and his family, along with his bachelor brother Arthur, were living at the family home Stottfield House in Hightown. Joshua Hartley Junior's private residence was Cawood Villa, in select Barnes Road.

In 1898 the company purchased the adjacent Phillips Pottery; it was then regarded as a nuisance, for it was also mining fireclay for their pots on property adjoining the brick works. At first there was no enthusiasm to keep this business working but it thrived after Joshua sent his sixteen year old nephew Herbert Lawrence Hartley, who had been firing the brick kilns, to supervise the firing of the pottery kilns. In the proceeding years the company began to expand and came to dominate the manufacturing of bricks in Castleford. In the mid 1890s the company purchased the established Redhill Brick Works on Eastfield Lane, which had been worked by Robert McDowall in 1875. In 1906 they purchased their third works, the disused Cawood Brick and Tile Company, near Selby, sixteen miles away from Castleford. In 1918 they also acquired the Healdfield Brick Company Limited, a company established in 1897 and sited in Cemetery Lane, later called Healdfield Road.

In 1893, prior to the acquisition of the brick works Joshua Hartley and Company was featured in a prestigious book, *The Century's Progress*, an illustrated book on Yorkshire Commerce, profiling the major cities and the smaller towns. Its inclusion is an indication of the status of the Castleford company. The article from this text is included below.

**Joshua Hartley & Co., Manufacturers of Sanitary Tubes, Chimney-tops, Terra-cotta Fire-bricks, & Company,** *Victoria Clay Works, Castleford.- This business has been in existence for a period of more than forty years, operations having been originally commenced in 1850 by Mr. Joshua Hartley in conjunction with Mr. George Turner Taylor, under the title of Joshua Hartley & Co. On the death of the latter gentleman Mr. Hartley remained alone at the head of affairs, and developed the concern with notable ability and success. He died in 1877, and was succeeded by his two sons - Messrs. C. J. and J. Hartley - who are the present sole proprietors, trading under the old and respected designation. The premises occupied cover an area of eight and a half acres. The main buildings comprise a compact suite of offices, show-room and various store-rooms, and there are, besides, extensive kilns (Hoffman's patent), brick-making sheds, moulding-sheds and every necessary department. The equipment has been carried out on a liberal scale, and includes all the latest plant and time-saving appliances known to the trade. Ample accommodation for sorting and forwarding purposes is possessed in the shape of a siding on the North Eastern Railway, and wharf on the Aire and Calder Navigation. From thirty to forty hands are employed, and extensive trade is being done in the manufacture of bricks for building purposes, quarries, red bricks, also pan tiles, drain tiles, ridge tiles. Immense quantities of these bricks are turned out, their superior quality insuring them ready sales. It should be noted that the whole of the clay used in these works is obtained on the premises, thus enabling the firm to quote such prices as can not be duplicated elsewhere. A leading line is* *made of sanitary tubing and chimney-tops. These are turned out in various sizes and in the latest and most approved shapes, well finished work being always guaranteed. Terra-cotta and firebricks are also made, by a special process, and are very much in demand among users of a better-class article. The proprietors give the business the full benefit of their long experience and matured skill, and a connection of great value has been developed, extending to every part of Yorkshire and to many of the adjacent counties, among the leading builders and contractors, railway companies, and collieries. Messrs C. J and J. Hartley enjoy the respect and esteem of all who know them, whether as the representatives of this branch of industry or as private citizens.*

During the early 1920s the company Joshua Hartley and Company, shifted its head quarters to the County Chambers in Bradley Street. This building had previously been the old police station, and was by then the office of their brother Arthur Hartley, architect and surveyor. In 1924 the family business became a limited company, operating as Hartleys (Castleford) Limited, with Charles and Joshua as managing directors. Just two years later in January 1926, at the age of seventy-two, Charles Hartley died at Stottfield House, Hightown.

Like most of the Hartley family Charles contributed to the social and industrial development of Castleford and Whitwood district through public service. In the early 1870s he was a founder member of the Castleford Rugby Football Club and was the chairman of the Urban Council as well as a local magistrate. During his life he was associated with many public offices and was chairman of the directors of the Claughton Manor Brick Company Limited, near Lancaster. Joshua subsequently became the managing director and chairman of the company and also a director of the Claughton Manor Brick Company Limited.

By 1934 the Redhill Brick Works had ceased production when it ran out of clay because it couldn't expand its boundaries due to being enclosed on all sides by the railway line, housing and the cemetery. However the company continued to invest and develop the pottery side of the business. In August 1934 they made a revolutionary development, they changed from using the traditional bottle-oven kilns to putting down a new type of tunnel kiln, the Dressler Oven, unique in this country.

In the following March Joshua, aged seventy-six, died at his home 'Castledene', Pontefract Road. Like his brothers, Joshua had been active in business and public life within the Castleford community. He had been a life long member of the Powell Street Methodist Church. His

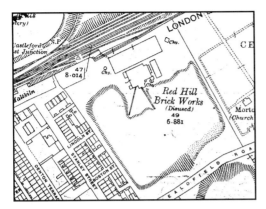

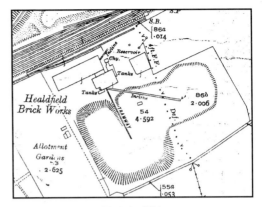

This map of 1934 shows the disused Redhill Brick Works.

The Healdfield Brick Works in 1934.

family had been founder members in the 1850s. In his younger days he was a keen sportsman and was instrumental in pioneering soccer in Castleford in the 1870s when it was not known in Yorkshire.

Joshua was succeeded as managing director by his nephew, Herbert Lawrence Hartley, who had been in charge of the Phillips Pottery. Joshua's son, John William Hartley, took over the managing of the brick making side of the company.

By the late 1930s there were only three remaining brick manufacturers in Castleford. Competition to Hartleys came from Charles Hattan who owned the Oxford Street Brickworks and the Yorkshire Brick Company Limited, on Leeds Road, Glasshoughton.

By 1947 another of the company's works, the Cawood Brick and Tile Works, subject to flooding, had stopped producing. However, the pottery side of the business continued to produce a wide variety of domestic household wares in the traditional blackware and stoneware. In the early 1950s the pottery introduced new types and ranges of ware to compete in the post-war market. In 1956, aged seventy, the company's managing director Herbert Lawrence Hartley died. Like his family predecessors he was popular with his work force and in the business community. He contributed greatly to the town being a Justice of

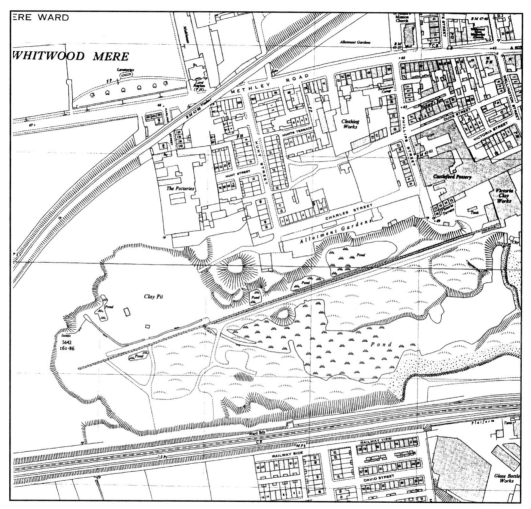

This map from 1953 shows the enclosed position of the Victoria Clay Works and its extensively quarried clay pit which was surrounded by Methley Road, the local housing and the railway lines.

the Peace and Chairman of the West Riding Magistrates at Castleford. He also served as a local councillor and was Chairman of the former Whitwood Urban District Council. His son, Frank Hartley, succeeded him as the company managing director.

Brick production remained relatively stable until the mid 1950s. Then Castleford Borough Council implemented a project of the mass clearance of old slum housing. In 1956 its policy was to build brick houses of the traditional type to cope with the very large council house building programme. At that time around three hundred new houses a year were being erected in the district. This resulted in new large out-of-town council housing estates being built. Love Lane, Half Acres, Whitwood, Airedale, Smawthorne and Ferry Fryston appeared, the latter estate alone had 2,800 houses. The 1950s and 1960s were busy decades for the brick making side of the company, however the pottery side was dying. Hartleys' Phillips Pottery closed in 1960.

During these busy times the company also lost a valued family member and director when in July 1963 John William Hartley died at the age of 76. Bill, as he was known, was associated with the brick manufacturing side of the business all his life. In his time he was a local sports man, playing bowls and tennis, but his passion was Rugby Union. In this game he was both a keen player and referee. For thirty years he was president of the Castleford Rugby Union Club.

In 1965 the company was brought under the sole ownership of Frank Hartley. By 1966 the Council had built a staggering 5,600 houses in the borough and had plans for more. This coupled with the Council's warden scheme for sheltered housing for the elderly, and the demand in the private housing building sector, meant the brickyards were once again booming. To meet this new demand it meant Hartleys had to increase its brick production. To maintain stable prices and be competitive the company installed a new brick making plant at the Victoria Clay Works in 1965/6. Inside the adjacent pottery in an area that had once housed the old tunnel kiln a Fawcett-Steele 60F Extrusion Unit was installed. This machine had been developed in America but at the time was manufactured by Thomas C Fawcett Limited, of Leeds. With ancillary equipment the press cost over £50,000. The unit had the potential to double the output and departed from the traditional methods of making bricks by the 'stiff plastic' method. By the late 1960s the Victoria Clay Works had run out of clay to make bricks. For a time the company managed to keep on producing bricks by quarrying and transporting clay from their other works at Healdfield but since this was expensive and there was not enough clay to keep up the brick production the company ran into financial difficulties and Hartley (Castleford) Limited went into voluntary liquidation, closing down in 1969.

The industrial activity of quarrying at the various brickworks left physical and visual scars on the local landscape. However, some thirty years later those scars are healing and we are pleased to see reclaimed land being used for business and pleasure activities. The Cawood Brick and Tile Company, disused for many years, was sold in 1969 and was subsequently transformed into the Cawood Holiday Park, an ideal setting for camping, caravans and fishing.

In February 1971 in Wellington Street, the two large chimneys, landmarks for the Victoria Clay Works, one rising to a height of a hundred and fifty feet and the other to two hundred feet high, crashed to the ground, brought down by gelignite charge. The works was subsequently demolished and was purchased by United Glass Containers, originally John Lumb's Limited. The huge clay quarry, which is now covered by scrub land, was used as a refuse tip and eventually filled with domestic and industrial waste. Today the whole site, that included the brick works and the Phillips Pottery, is covered in large warehouses and is used by UCI Logistics, a haulage and distribution company.

Although now reclaimed there are still visible reminders of the Redhill and Healdfield brickworks. For as you travel eastwards along Healdfield Road a few old remaining buildings of the Redhill Brickworks still stand. These are used by a motor car scrap yard. The extent of the clay extraction is clearly visible for there is a deep depression left on the adjacent land, which is the sports field of Castleford High School Technology College. Further along the road, on the site of the Healdfield Brickworks, the large clay quarry has been filled with industrial waste by Hargreaves, and recently landscaped into a public space. At the old entrance to the brick works, a large stone has been erected, inscribed 'Hartleys Field'.

## HARTLEYS (CASTLEFORD) LTD.

### (ESTABLISHED 1848)

Telephone 2262, 2586

COLOURED
SANDFACED                         SELECTED
RUSTIC FACED                      ENGINEERS
– – – – – **BRICKS** – – – – –
COMMON                            SPECIALS

Office & Works :                  Works :
**VICTORIA CLAY WORKS,**          **HEALDFIELD BRICKWORKS,**
**WELLINGTON STREET,**            **HEALDFIELD ROAD,**
**WHITWOOD MERE,**                **CASTLEFORD**
**CASTLEFORD**

Top, the Healdfield Brick Works taken in 1969. Left, John William Hartley (1887-1963) the eldest son of Joshua Hartley (Jnr). Right, a mid 1960s advert from Castleford Handbook, shows the range of bricks being made from their two Castleford works.

This view of the Redhill Brickworks was taken from the Castleford Sketch Book of local artist Albert Wainwright, dated 1928. The scene was painted from Healdfield Road looking northwards towards Wheldon Road. The foreground shows tramway tracks leading into the preparation workshops from the quarry. The brick kiln can be seen to the left behind the workshops. The workshop building is still in use as a motor car scrap dealership. The quarry has been filled and is now Castleford High School Technology College playing field.

# BRICK MAKING

Terry Gill started work at the Victoria Clay Works in the early 1950s and worked there until its closure in the late 1960s. His recollections give us a detailed account of brick making during those decades.

## Clay Winning and Preparation

*The quarry at the Victoria Clay Works was of great extent and excavated to a depth of around sixty feet. To the latter part of the quarry's life the methods of clay extraction had not changed much from the olden days. The clay was detached from the quarry face by drilling a series of holes and shot-firing using detonators and explosives. When advancing in the quarry we worked from a loose end, working in sections at a time, this system of working we called benching. Prior to firing the quarry face certain bands of impurities such as coal, a hard black rock called blacks, and fire clay had to be removed. They were not needed in the mixture. The coal and the blacks were broke up and lifted manually by hand using iron crow bars and shovels. The coal was saved and used to fuel the kiln, the blacks discarded.*

*Underneath the blacks laid a band of fire clay; this was extracted using a digger pick, removed from the site, stock piled or sent up for use in the pottery. Once the impurities had been removed the quarry face was fired. The blue clay at the bottom would blow first, then the middle section, then the upper soils, all mixing together in a large heap on the ground. The side had to be fired like this, or we didn't get the perfect mix for the Hartley brick. The texture and quality had to be right. A good blowing could give us enough work hand-filling to last a week.*

*Powered by an old steam engine that was housed in the machine shop above in the brick yard, the clay was transported up to the works in steel tubs that ran on narrow gauge tramway tracks. These tubs were attached to an endless chain haulage system called a 'ginny'. The ginny had a stationary return-wheel at the bottom of*

The ginny haulage system in use at the Doncaster Brick Company Limited. It was a common method of transportation of clay from the quarries.

the quarry and the tracks stopped there. To retrieve clay from the different areas of the quarry we would lay down temporary tracks. The empty tubs were then filled by hand, using picks and shovels. Each tub held about six hundred weight. The fully laden tubs were then pushed back along the temporary track and linked up to the endless chain haulage which hauled them up to the brickyard. When the tubs reached the yard a lad had the job of spinning the tub off, tipping the contents into the bottom pan, and returning the empty tub back down into the quarry.

The bottom pan was a type of mill, circular in construction that has two large six feet steel rollers revolving on a stationary base, crushing and kneading the clays with the natural soils. The clay then passed through perforated grates in the bottom of the pans and onto a chute. It was then elevated to the top floor of the works to go in to the top pan. Here again it was ground, and water was added to achieve a finer texture. The clay once again passed through smaller grates in the top pan and down into the spout. At this point it was the job of a young lad to ensure the clay trickled consistently. In that way it fed the pug mill.

## Shaping and Moulding

The pug mill was an integral part of the brick making machine. It churned and kneaded the clay using a series of knives upon a rotating shaft and then extruded the clay onto a circular machine table which held around thirty brick moulds which had been coated with a thick black oil. The pug mill forced the clay into the moulds and produced a roughly pressed shaped brick.

The automated machine then lifted the brick and transferred it to another part of the machine to be re-pressed. There the lettering was stamped on and it was finished to the required standard. The brick at this stage was called a green brick, for it was in its raw state. The bricks were next released automatically from their moulds and stacked by men on to wooden boards on a tub. This was called 'hugging off'.

We also made special bricks by hand, such as half round, bull nosed, octagons, and sill-bricks. Hand moulding was done in a little shed near the fitter's

The old production methods as used at Hartleys, were still in use at the Normanton Brick Company in 1997. On the left is a brick making machine, it shows the green brick being pushed up from the circular plate after its first pressing. After pressing the bricks are 'hugged off' on to a wheel barrow for transportation to the kiln.

*shop. For a run of these specials bricks, extra water was applied in the mixing pan, for a softer textured clay was needed. I would take 50 or 100 initial pressed bricks from the machine shop on a barrow to the small shed. There the soft brick was cut to shape and placed into a singular wooden mould and bits of clay were added to finally give the correct shape. The mould was then put under a hand press, which had a large counter weight on top. As you swung it round it applied pressure, pressing the brick. The brick was released from the mould by an arm, operated by a foot pedal. The bricks were then placed on a wooden board to dry off. If a good red engineering brick finish was required I would coat the face and sides with a bitumen tar, this gave each a good red finish when it had been baked. These types of bricks were expensive to make and to buy.*

*The fully laden tubs were then pushed out of the main doors across the yard to the kiln along a tramway, which encircled the outside of the whole kiln. This procedure was called tramming. The tub of bricks was then pushed to the entrance of the kiln's firing chamber, called the wicket hole.*

Green bricks being wheel-barrowed in to the entrance of the chamber through the wicket hole of the kiln at Normanton Brickworks in 1997.

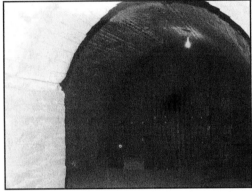

The firing chamber partly filled with green bricks. Normanton Brickworks 1997.

## The Kilns

*At Hartleys Victoria Clay Works in Whitwood Mere there were two kilns. The largest was a Hoffman Kiln. This was rectangular in shape with rounded ends. In the centre of the kiln was a tall brick chimney. The kiln had fourteen burning chambers.*

*This differed from the smaller rectangular kiln which had twelve firing chambers.*

*Each chamber could hold 13,000 to 14,000 bricks at a time. The chambers on the corners of the larger kiln were bigger and could hold 3,000 to 4,000 more bricks. Each of the chambers was divided by a brick partition. Access to each chamber was through a brick archway called a wicket hole. A system of flues led from the chambers to a tall central chimney. Each chamber was set, dried, burnt, cooled and emptied in sequence moving in a clockwise direction. The firing zone is advanced round the kiln by opening the flue dampers ahead in turn. In those days on top of each chamber in the crown was a small feed hole, through which slack coal is fed to sustain the fire and heat. The kiln was in continuous use twenty-four hours a day.*

*Placing the bricks inside the chambers was the job of the setters. The tub of green bricks was derailed and pushed inside the chamber onto large sheets of steel plates, making it an easier and faster unloading operation. Generally it took three men to unload the tub and set the bricks for firing. The setters skilfully stacked the bricks on end, ensuring the bricks were evenly spaced apart. A finger space was about enough to allow the coal to burn, and the fire gases and heat to circulate evenly. This work also involved putting down draught and flue lines in a set pattern for the coal to burn. There was an art in setting but you also had to use some common sense and occasionally make adjustments. Different quality bricks were placed in different parts of the chamber. For the heat distribution favoured some more than others. One-course in, on the side of the chamber, you placed the soft bricks, these are what we called an imperfect brick, the sort used for common building work. In the centre of the chamber was placed the best engineering brick, a hard red, high quality brick. Later on we introduced other types of bricks called Autumn Browns and Rustics. These went through a machine that sand blasted them with silica-sand. I used to go in the wagon all the way down south to Leighton Buzzard for it. This was the only place you could get it from. The Autumn Browns and the Rustics fired best placed in the centre of the chamber. We would do a run of around 6,000 to 8,000 of them at a time.*

## Firing

*Once the chamber had been set and was full, the yard-lad built up the wicket hole, sealing it with old bricks and rendering the face with a mixture of ash and clay to give an air tight seal. The bricks were then left in the chamber to thoroughly dry out before they could be fired. Heat from the neighbouring chamber enhanced the drying, this generally took around two days. To fire the chamber, heat was drawn through a flue system by opening dampers leading the heat to the chamber. This allowed the fuel spaced between the bricks to burn. Coal was also fed into the chamber from on top of the kiln through small feed holes left by the kiln-top men.*

The setter at work stacking bricks in the chamber at Normanton Brickworks in 1997.

Rendering up the wicket hole of the chamber. The bricks were left to dry-out using heat from the kiln prior to firing at Normanton Brickworks in 1997.

*A couple of shovels full of coal were fed in at a time and these continuously fuelled the fire and created the intense red hot heat required to bake the bricks. To change the raw green bricks into hard bricks they had to burn at a bright red heat at a temperature 950-1150 degrees centigrade; 1742-2102 degrees Fahrenheit. The bricks generally took around seven to eight days to bake, then the dampers were closed off, and the kiln was left to cool down. It was then the job of the Drawers-Off to break down and open up the chamber's wicket hole, gain access, and withdraw the baked bricks.*

Opening the fire hole on top of the chamber at Normanton Brickworks in 1997.

The rendered wall taken down from the wicket hole of the chamber reveals the newly fired bricks at Normanton Brickworks in 1997.

This photograph, taken in 1965, shows the Victoria Clay Works, Whitwood Mere. Behind the chimney were the works preparation sheds. These were attached to the old pottery building in which the new brick making machine the Fawcett-Steele 60F Extrusion Unit was installed. The large elliptical Hoffmann Kiln had fourteen burning chambers and at its centre a chimney. Adjacent was the rectangular kiln which had twelve burning chambers.

*At this stage the bricks were still warm, and many too hot to touch, the hottest bricks being on the bottom rows or the ones at the back of the chamber. For protection, and to make handling easier, the drawers made themselves protective hand pads from thick rubber tubing. This covered the thumb and the palm of the hand.*

*Various modes of transport were applied over a time to empty the chamber. The old method was loading the bricks on to a wheel barrow. This work was time consuming for the barrow could only hold around 50 or 60 bricks. The most efficient method was the wheeled tub, this could be loaded inside the chamber and pushed along on steel sheets then engaged back onto rails outside the wicket. This method allowed us to load up to around 250 to 300 bricks at a time. Once the chamber had been emptied it was the job of the Kiln-lad to go in and clean out all the ash and broken bricks ready for the next setting, dumping all the debris in the quarry.*

Inside the chamber, drawing off the bricks at Normanton Brickworks in 1997.

A broadside view of the Normanton Brickworks kiln with the packed bricks outside the chambers ready for distribution in 1997.

*The new bricks were stock piled anywhere and everywhere around the yard. We had lorries which, loaded up, could hold 2000 to 2500 bricks at a time. A big 'artic' from one of the big builders, such as S A Bell or Sheppards, could carry 5000 bricks. Some bricks were transported by rail. To do this our lorries were loaded up and straw was lain between the bricks so as not to scratch the facings. They were then transported a short distance across Methley Road to a rail siding which was just behind the Pointer public house. The bricks were then unloaded off the lorry and reloaded on to the railway carriage. We supplied all the local building trade but our main distributers in the 1950s and 1960s, were the local councils. We had to make sure we had 8000 or 10,000 bricks of their choice ready for them at any time. Our bricks were in great demand being used in the building of the housing estates at Ferry Fryston, Half Acres and Whitwood.*

## Modern Methods

*The Hartley bricks made under the old traditional methods were of a high quality, a fact which showed in the demand. We sold as many as we could produce, and had full order books, but the old method of making bricks couldn't cope with the demand so in the late 1950s the Victoria Clay Works began to introduce new working methods. During this re-modernisation period the old system of chain haulage was taken out of the quarry and was replaced by heavy mechanical vehicles. Six four-wheeled ex-army lorries worked alongside a 22 RB excavator which was purchased for the quarry.*

*To cope with the demand in the mid 1960s a new wire cut brick making machine was installed in part of the old pottery buildings that once housed the tunnel kiln. The new machine made a different type of brick. They were lighter for it was perforated with holes and therefore used less clay. To make this type a large block of clay was extruded from the pug mill and was cut with a wire, just like cheese, leaving rows of shaped bricks. The bricks travelled on a conveyor where they were picked up by suction pads and transferred onto tubs. This method of working could mass produce 75,000-90,000 bricks a day if required. It also did away with some jobs, for it eliminated the need for the men who worked the top-pan.*

*To manage the firing of increased intense production we opened up a stagnant kiln at the Victoria Clay Works and an old kiln that had been closed for some time at the Healdfield Brickworks. At this time the Victoria Clay Works quarry, which had been supplying clay to the works for well over a hundred years, was beginning to run out. It was getting harder to quarry, for it was constricted by the fact that its boundary was the two railway lines and the Three Lane Ends housing estate. When the quarry dried up we re-opened the Healdfield Brickworks Quarry. The clay quarried at Healdfield Brickworks was far inferior to that at the Victoria Clay works. The clay was transported to the Victoria Clay Works by lorries to be pressed into bricks. The raw bricks were then transported back to the Healdfield Brickworks to be fired in the kiln. At this time, to meet demand, we had three kilns working.*

*Sometimes I was sent to work the pumps in the Victoria Clay Works quarry. It was always filling up with natural underground spring water that ran down the face of the quarry. It was clean and beautiful, second to none. We pumped it all in to the River Aire, except in the hot summer days, when we would make ourselves a swimming pool using the stock pile of fire clay and the ready supply of fresh spring water. We had water running in one end and running out the other.*

*Advancing the quarry created water ponds. After a while the ponds got stocked with pike, perch and tench. As we drained the ponds off we had to wade in and catch all the fish and put them in huge Ali-Baba type jars. They were then loaded on to a lorry and transported and released in the Cawood Works pond.*

*I reckon as a worker, that if we had of carried on producing bricks in the old method we would have been alright. It was progress and the new manufacturing methods, using a wire cut machine, that helped in the company's decline. In the end Hartleys brick works ceased production and closed in 1969.*

# Pot by Pot

# POTTERY LINEAGE

Castleford clays were recognised as of quality and quite distinctive within Yorkshire from the mid eighteenth century onwards. The pottery industry in Castleford used two types, earthenware and stoneware. Earthenware clay, sometimes called Blackware, is local clay found near to the surface and contains a large amount of iron. It may be brownish-red or greenish-grey in colour when extracted but fires to a red-brown and brownish-black. Stoneware clay is highly fired, ranging from 1200-1300 degrees centigrade, and as the name suggests that, like stone, it is strong, durable, dense and nonporous. When fired the colour ranges from white to buff.

For over two hundred years these types of clay were used to make pottery on the site of Phillips Pottery, so when the last owners of the pottery, Hartleys (Castleford) Limited, closed in 1960 the pottery had undergone change. It was the earliest pottery in the district. Proof of this unbroken industrial continuity occurred in 1935 when extensive alterations to the premises revealed a wooden roof beam that bore the date 1775. The extent of the quarrying behind the pottery was also an indication that extraction of clays had gone on for a long time.

The origin of the Phillips Pottery, later and better known as Hartleys, occurred around 1724 when John Clay purchased land south of Methley Road in Whitwood Mere, to manufacture bricks and tiles. The works was situated there because the raw material was readily available. This source was probably worked single handed in the early years so was on a small scale. At this time John Clay hand moulded the bricks and tiles, fired them in a primitive kiln, and supplied the local area as far as Pontefract and Wakefield. In the subsequent years he built up a good business with established brick and tile kilns. In the 1770s he sold the land and kilns to Thomas Brough who built it up into a small pottery. He in turn sold the pottery in 1783 for £170 to two Quakers, Nathanial English of Allerton Bywater and William Thompson, a Leeds merchant. The pottery at that time, known as the Castleford Mere Pottery, had workshops, warehouses and brick and tile kilns, and also a hovel kiln for burning pots. The English and Thompson partnership had grander ideas, so in 1784 they went on to purchase land and build another pottery and an oven for burning flint, on the north side of

Methley Road. That site abutted the River Calder, and the company manufactured a finer ware.

In August 1785 Thompson bought English's share of the two potteries and was joined by William Taylor, formerly of the Rothwell Pottery. In 1790, trading as William Taylor and Company, the two parts of the business, the finer-ware pottery and the brick and tile kilns, were sold to David Dunderdale and John Plowes. They traded as D. Dunderdale & Company and called their business Castleford Pottery. They continued to work both sides of the business producing coarseware pottery and bricks on the south side of Methley Road, and fineware on the north side. Sales bills survive showing bricks from the Castleford Pottery were supplied to build Warren House, a mansion in Warrengate, Wakefield. They were delivered in four boats along the River Calder. We know the price. Best bricks, plus delivery, cost 28 shillings a thousand. Some common bricks at 20 shillings a thousand were also purchased from the same source.

In the 1750s the staple English pottery, gracing the tables of the middle class families in this area and beyond, was called Creamware. These wares were made from imported finer quality clays. The riverside position of the pottery, essential for the entrepreneurs, shipped coal for firing the kilns and clays from Devon, Cornwall and Dorset and brought it in by barge from the ports of Hull and Selby. Flint came from Sussex to be ground to make the glazes. Dunderdale's pottery quickly expanded and in that phase changed from a domestic pottery to a factory one. Dunderdale exported much of his creamware to Spain, America and France. In 1796 he was so conscious of marketing that he published the Castleford Pottery Pattern Book, illustrating 259 Creamware shapes.

In the early 1800s the tableware fashion changed again and Dunderdale diversified into making transfer-printed Pearlware. This ware had a similar body to the Creamware but had a greater percentage of flint and china clay, the glazes, containing cobalt, gave a bluish finish. A transfer pattern Dunderdale used prolifically on this ware was called Buffalo and Ruins. The pottery was also renowned for its distinctive tea pots. These were made from white felspathic stoneware, and ornamented with classical figures, often outlined in blue. A range of black basalt tea pots was also made.

It was not all plain sailing. In 1803 John Plowes was declared bankrupt and left the pottery. Two years later he joined in partnership with his son at the Ferrybridge Pottery. Dunderdale in turn took on new partners, Thomas Russell of Leeds, Thomas Upton, and John Bramley also from Leeds. The coarseware pottery on the south side of Methley Road continued to make earthenware, bricks and tiles and was managed by Thomas Steven Russell, son of one of the pottery partners.

During the Peninsular War (1808-1814) Napoleon had closed all European ports to British traders. This French action brought about a huge loss of revenue to the Castleford Pottery. Mounting debts, coupled with a general slump in the country's economy in the post-war years, meant the pottery never recovered and was forced to close in 1821. The closure of one pottery revitalised others of the Castleford pottery industry and after a time business picked up. The coarseware pottery on the south side of Methley Road continued to manufacture under Thomas Steven Russell. The large vacant fineware pottery on the north of the road was split up and sold off to former workmen to make three individual potteries. These had a succession of owners between 1821 and 1883. Eventually, all three separate potteries came under one ownership and took the name Clokie & Company.

A selection of Dunderdale pottery shows a lattice basket, stand and plates of the earlier Creamware. The jug is in Pearlware.
The pottery David Dunderdale established is renowned world wide as producing high quality wares. His pieces of pottery are very rare and therefore command high prices to collectors.

# MERE POTTERY 1821-1935

After the dissolution of Dunderdale's Castleford Pottery, the coarseware pottery was owned by Thomas Steven Russell. A trade directory of 1822 shows that Russell was producing stoneware products. Russell remained at the pottery until the late 1830s and was succeeded by John Bateson and Company. Bateson was a businessman who had also built another coarseware pottery nearby. In 1838 the pottery was still making stone and blackware products. During the 1840s the pottery was purchased by Thomas Wilson and James Harling who traded as Wilson, Harling and Company. The Ordnance Survey Map of 1846 calls this coarseware pottery Mere Pottery.

In 1849, Wilson & Harling took on another partner, Charles Phillips, and traded under the name Harling & Phillips. Wilson and Harling also built another pottery in 1852 situated in Harling Street. This was south of Methley Road, near to where the old Whitwood Branch line crossed the road. Many years later this pottery traded as Henry Bradshaw and Son. Thomas Wilson retired in 1861 and soon after, in 1863, the partnership of Harling and Phillips was dissolved. At that point the two potteries were split. Harling keeping the pottery he had established in Harling Street and Charles Phillips the Mere Pottery. Phillips was joined by his son in 1878 and the new firm became C. Phillips & Son. By this time the pottery had become a large concern within Castleford.

The pottery, sited along Phillips Street, was medium sized as potteries go, rectangular in shape and consisted of mostly single storey buildings. The clay preparation area was situated at the bottom of the pottery near to the quarry. It had two traditional style bottle-cone shaped ovens, often called kilns by the workers. One kiln was used for firing stoneware products, the other for blackware products. As the population of Whitwood Mere expanded, the pottery became hemmed in on all sides by terraced housing; to the north was Duke Street, to the east Victoria Street, in the west Phillips Street and to the south of the pottery a clay quarry.

At the end of the 1890s the Phillips Pottery used a process of taking the basic raw clay, adding water and refining into a mixture called slip. To get the slip to the proper consistency they had to entirely remove all the foreign matter. This was achieved by rubbing the slip, by hand through silk, a long tedious process. A reference from an old employee in 1935 recalls how, as a boy, he was sent to a mercers in Castleford to buy silk by the yard for this very process. The slip was then dried out in large drying pans heated from underneath by coal. The clay was then stamped on by the workmen and piled up for a few days in heaps to become 'sour' and left to ferment. The next process was to put it through the pug mill. This compressed it, taking all the air out and making the clay a perfectly solid mass ready for use. Early in the twentieth century this type of labour-intense preparation was superseded by the introduction of steam, and later, electricity powered machinery.

Moving with the times, Charles Phillips introduced innovative changes into the pottery when he implemented the up-grading of the pottery lighting system. Where previously the workers worked by flickering candlelight he introduced oil lamps that hung on the walls. Around 1895 the pottery purchased, from a brickworks in York, a steam engine made by Manning Wardle & Company, Leeds. It was the first steam engine to be used in any Yorkshire pottery. It revolutionised the pottery for it produced a new whole power system. It generated the energy to work the throwing wheels and other machinery which had previously been powered by hand. By the 1930s the pottery was illuminated by electricity.

The pottery extracted fire clays to manufacture household goods from the land behind the works. Adjacent to the pottery since the 1850s was the Victoria Clay Works, owned by the Hartley family. They quarried for clay from behind their works to manufacture items for the building trade. In the 1890s Joshua and Charles were directors of the company and the brick works traded under Joshua Hartley & Company. Hartleys regarded the neighbouring pottery as something of a nuisance and eventually negotiated a take-over in 1899. Initially there was not a great deal of enthusiasm, but when Joshua sent in his sixteen year old nephew Lawrence Hartley, who had previously been firing the brick kilns, to superintend the firing of the pottery kilns, there was a change in attitude. The change from producing proaic house bricks to the more glamorous domestic article aroused an enthusiasm which Lawrence Hartley maintained for fifty years.

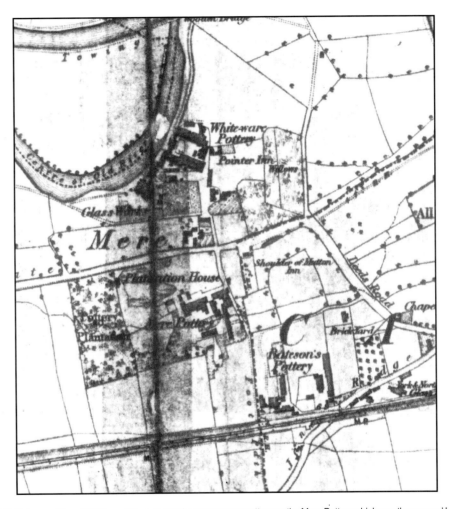

This 1846 Ordnance Map of Whitwood Mere shows the coarseware pottery as the Mere Pottery which was then owned by Wilson & Harling Co. It was situated south of Methley Road as was the nearby Batesons Pottery, which bounders on to the railway line.

This photograph, taken in 1926, shows the Phillips Pottery that was situated on Phillips Street, Whitwood Mere, being bound in on three sides by terrace housing. The pottery was rectangular in shape. The cone shaped stoneware kiln can clearly be seen in the centre of the pottery buildings.

# A CONTEMPORARY ACCOUNT OF THE POTTERY-1893

A summary of the pottery was included in a prestigious edition of the 1893 book *The Century's Progress*. This profiles Yorkshire commerce. The account below gives a good contemporary account of the pottery at the height of its power.

**C. Phillips & Son, Manufacturers of Stone Bottles and Jars,** *Castleford -The pioneer firm engaged in the bottle and jar manufacturing industry, which now, in its various branches, forms one of the staple trades of the Castleford district, is in all probability that which is represented by Messrs C. Phillips & Son. The extensive business which they conduct, with exceptionally intelligent enterprise, was founded by Mr Russell upwards of half a century ago, and during the many years of his control he was successful in creating the nucleus of the valuable connection which has since been solidified and expanded by those who have come after him. In the case of such a distinctly representative house as that under notice, it is well to place on record the unbroken commercial lineage which connects its past and its present. Mr Russell was succeeded by Messrs Bateson, who again were succeeded by Messrs Harling & Wilson, they being in 1849 joined the senior partner of the existing firm, Mr C. Phillips. The style and title of the house then became Messrs Harling & Phillips, and so continued until 1860, when the former gentleman retired, and the business was continued by Mr Phillips alone until 1878. He was then joined by his son, when the present style was adopted. The premises of the firm cover a large area. At the entrance is a detached building, comprising a suite of well appointed general and private offices, with every requisite for the prompt despatch of the large amount of clerical work necessitated by the numerous and important transactions of the firm. The commodious works include throwing and drying rooms, fine baking-kilns, packing-rooms and a spacious warehouse in which are always held large stocks of the various productions of the firm. Their business consists in the manufacture of black and stone ware, for which the house obtained a very high reputation in the market. Their stoneware includes all sorts of stone bottles and jars for the use of wine and spirits merchants (many of the bottles for these trades being wicker cased), druggists, drysalters, and jam and pickle manufacturers. In addition to their stoneware, which forms the speciality of the firm, they are also large manufacturers of blackware, including bowls for kitchen and domestic use. The house have an extensive and ever-widening connection, which extends all over the United Kingdom amongst wholesale and retail dealers, and also among the several trades enumerated above. So excellent are all the appliances for the production* *of the firm's specialities, and so skilful and experienced their large staff of workmen, that Messrs C. Phillips & Son are able to compete successfully with any house in their own line of business in the country. As befits the representatives of a great pioneer industry, the members of the firm take an active interest in the public life of the district. Mr Charles Phillips, the senior partner is chairman of the Whitwood Local Board, and an overseer of the Pontefract Union Board. Mr Charles Arthur Phillips, the sleeping partner, is a solicitor, and holds the position of clerk to the Whitwood Local Board, the Whitwood, Glass Houghton, and the Kippax School Boards. Mr Charles Phillips, the senior partner, assisted by Mr Fredrick Rice Phillips, takes the entire practical management of the commercial and industrial departments of the business, in which from thirty-five to forty hands are regularly employed, and to him belongs much of the credit for the continued extension of the firm's influence.*

The cone or bottle shaped ovens were a striking feature of the pottery environment. These evolved from medieval and post-medieval kilns in which the pots were placed separate from the heat and the surrounding fire boxes. By the end of the seventeenth century this type of kiln was occasionally surrounded by a hovel, an outer brick shell, which encased and protected the oven and acted as a chimney to control and direct the draught upwards. These requirements created the characteristic bottle outline shape. They were built in many shapes and sizes and were familiar to all who knew the potteries in Castleford.

At Phillips Pottery two down-draught ovens were used. The principle of this oven was that the hot air rose up inside the oven and was forced back down and out through a hole in the centre of the floor of the oven. Smoke rose through a chimney nearby. The stoneware oven utilised the boiler house chimney. Here the excess heat was utilised by channelling it through underground flues to heat drying sheds. The blackware oven was sited in a single storey building and had a shorter chimney some distance away. The ovens were built of brick and were enclosed and incorporated within the buildings so that only the top portion of the stack emerged above the workshop roof.

## WORKER'S ACCOUNTS

Below former worker, Wilf Beedle, recalls his early days at the pottery.

*I started work at the pottery in 1930, following the family tradition, just like my father and grandfather before me, I became a potter at Phillips Pottery. It was my father who got me the job, for I had already secured a job working on the screens on the surface at Glasshoughton Colliery, but he said to me 'tha's going to no pit, tha starts at Hartleys on Monday'. I was his apprentice and he taught me the trade just as he was taught by his father back at the turn of the century. My grandfather worked at Hartleys until he was seventy-five.*

*My first job was as an assistant in the warehouse. Everything that came out of the two kilns I had to inspect, dress, sort and size before it went into the appropriate areas. Early in the job someone chucked me an old rubber inner tube and said, 'Make yourself some hand protectors'. This essential item was made with two slits to put your hand through and one for the thumb. With this you could handle the freshly fired pottery. Sharp edges cut your hands to ribbons.*

*The raw clay we used at the pottery was extracted from the quarry using explosives. The first strata layer of the quarry was soil, under that laid a snuff-coloured clay called blackware, next came a seam of coal that overlaid the stoneware clay. This was grey in colour and had a depth of eight to nine feet.*

*When extruding was about to begin large, flat steel sheets were laid on the ground as near to the newly exposed clay as possible. Derailed tubs would then be pushed along to gain access to the clay. The fully laden tubs were then pushed back along the sheets and engaged on to the track and coupled to the haulage system. From there they were sent up to the brickyard and the preparation shop. When that was reached the full tub was tipped on its side, emptying its contents on the ground behind the blunger house. From here the clay was wheelbarrowed to be mixed in the blunger.*

*The two large blungers were steel tanks measuring around six feet wide by five feet deep. Inside the blunger was a central revolving spindle to which was attached sharp blades. These cut through the raw clay kneading through a stirring motion. With expertise it was mixed. There were so many barrows full of clay, to so much water. This process went on until the mixture became a slip which had the consistency of Yorkshire pudding mixture. The mixing process took around one hour. The slip was then drained off from the blungers into two large sieves, one for each blunger. As I remember the sieves were suspended from old bits of belting and swung in a rocking motion, the mixture strained through the sieves which removed all the large lumps and other impurities. Traces of metal were extracted with magnets.*

*The slip was then funnelled off into two under floor tanks. From the tanks it was pumped up to be cleaned once again, this time through an electric sieve which had three different size 'lawn', that is brass wire mesh. The sieves were sloped so the slip ran through the largest size mesh on to the middle size then finally through the finest sieve. This had one hundred and twenty meshes to the inch. Finally the slip collected in another tank.*

*In the next process you removed all the water from the slip. This was done in the press shop. There were six different sized filter presses. The liquid slip was pumped into a press. This machine resembled a concertina. The press consisted of a series of rectangular, concave steel sheets abutted in a row, with each having a hole in its centre through which passed a pipe which forced the slip between the sheets. Canvas sheets, a touch larger than the steel press sheets, were placed between the plates and stabilising rods which ran through the canvas sheets, holding them up. This press held up to thirty steel plates. It was filled with the slip which created a large sandwich: steel plate, canvas sheet, slip, canvas sheet, and steel plate. This relationship continued all along the central column. Pressure was applied to the large sandwich through a screw thread pressure plate.*

*The press was left overnight for the excess water to drain off, leaving the slip to solidify. On release the pressure plate left the solid blocks of clay which measured three foot by four foot. These blocks were then put in to a pug mill which resembled a mincing machine. It had rotating blades inside that kneaded the clay, removed all the air bubbles, and give it its uniform plasticity. The processed clay was extruded on to a wooden board where it was stacked; one side for blackware the other for stoneware. It was left there until Bill Oxberry and Ernie Maskill cut off the required amount for the thrower or the jollier.*

*Radiating around the base of the stoneware kiln were twenty or thirty firing holes. This was where the coal was fed in to keep the oven burning. The firing was a 24 hour non-stop process of wheel barrowing coal to feed the fires. Above the firing holes on the first floor was the entrance in to the kiln. Steel bands around the whole of the oven had a stabilising function. They expanded as the kiln warmed up and contracted as the kiln cooled down.*

*The manufactured pottery wares were placed in clay boxes called saggars. The saggar was a circular container made of fireclay into which the ware was placed as a protection from the direct action of the flames and gasses during firing.*

*In my day the saggar-maker was a Staffordshire chap who had his own shop where he made the saggars but eventually a new machine shop building was created for the making of saggar clay. I recall it had white tiled walls and a red tiled floor on which a diesel engine was installed to drive a grinding machine. Inside the machine were two large metal wheels that ran opposite ways from each other. Stoneware clay and old broken saggars were placed into the machine to be ground. A long metal shovel was used to turn over the ground clay as it came from under the grinding wheels until a good pliable texture was obtained. The clay, or marl, was then loaded into a wheelbarrow and taken to the saggar shop.*

*Inside the saggar shop, on a large bench, was a rectangular metal frame. The marl was placed into this and beaten to the shape of the frame with a large wooden mallet. Occasionally we would add a little sawdust to stop the mallet sticking to the marl. Once flat and when the correct depth had been achieved the marl was placed on a round wooden drum template and cut to length. The two ends were then joined together. Another template was used to shape the bottom of the saggar. The bottom and the side of the saggar was placed on a turning wheel and joined together. The saggers were then fired in the oven before they could be used.*

*It was the job of the kiln setters to stack the saggars in the kiln. The saggars were placed in the kiln in a concentric circle pattern, right to the top. We recognised that the closer the saggars were packed the longer it took to fire them. Before firing the kilns, the entrance hole was built up using fire bricks plastered with clay and slurry to give a tight seal. The fire, in the bottom half of the kiln, was ignited using the hot ashes from the old steam boiler. The full kiln was then fully fired and fed with coal through the twenty to thirty firing holes that radiated around the kiln base. During the firing the kiln was attended 24 hours a day, men continuously supplying the fire with fuel. It took around three days to bake the pottery. Generally we started on from Wednesday and the process was over by Saturday afternoon.*

*In the old blackware kiln we fired bowls, cream pots and bread pots. In these cases not many saggars were used for we could use rings and quarries. These rings were made of clay and were manufactured from one of the machines we used for making handles for the jugs. The rings were glazed so the pottery wouldn't stick to them. The rings had a lip on them which fitted over the pot so that they could be stacked. In the blackware kiln were quarries which were stacked to make a type of cupboard. On shelves, around three feet long by one feet wide, the bread pots and cream pots were placed to be fired.*

An advert from around 1920. Although Hartleys owned the pottery it retained the previous owners name, C Phillips & Son.

Inside one of Clokie & Company Ltd. bottle oven kilns. This would have been very similar to the kilns at Hartleys. The setters are stacking saggars, containers which are full of pieces of pottery. The hole in the floor under the ladder is where the heat escapes.

# MODERNISATION

The bottle ovens that had served the pottery for well over a hundred years were replaced in 1934 by the revolutionary deployment of a new type of kiln, the Dressler Oven, sometimes referred to as the Gibbons Oven. The one installed in the pottery years ago was unique to this country at that time. The new kiln had many advantages over the bottle ovens for the ware did not need saggers. Nor did the kiln have to be kept fuelled for days on end and drawn off after firing. The extremely hot, hard and dirty work therefore almost disappeared overnight. The new kiln produced a higher output of quality goods, it also made a cleaner environment. That was because it used a producer gas piped from the Coke Works in Glasshoughton. Later the kiln was converted to use the town's gas.

The ware went into the new Dressler Kiln stacked upon five and a half feet long trucks one by one entering at one end and emerging at the other end two hundred feet away. The trucks proceeded through the kiln in a cool atmosphere moving so slowly that movement could barely be observed, passing along through a temperature from 1,080 degrees centigrade to 1,260 degrees centigrade. Thirty hours later the articles were perfectly baked and glazed. Along the outside of the kiln a series of spy holes allowed a worker to check the truck's passage. On the odd occasion while travelling through the kiln an item of pottery would move while on the truck, or sometimes it touched the sides of the kiln. This caused further distribution to the other laden pottery. To dislodge the stuck item Mr Cheesbrough used a 2.2 rifle. He shot through the spy hole, smashing the offending piece and releasing the truck.

The pottery also used a second, but smaller, gas fired enamel kiln of the intermittent type. It was devised and constructed by the company's own engineers and operated on the radiant heat principle, its top temperature was 720 degrees centigrade. It was principally used for firing earthenware on-glaze enamels, but also for stoneware mugs and beakers. These had been introduced, purely for experimental purposes, to test fire bone-china enamels. The company didn't make bone-china although they successfully discovered a kiln which could cope with highly specialised ware.

The truck of earthenware mugs and beakers ready to enter the small gas-fired enamel kiln to be fired. It was used to fire glazes onto items of pottery that didn't need the extreme heat of the tunnel kiln. White glaze was a softer glaze than the stone glaze so it didn't need as much firing, but it still gave just the right temperature to fuse the gold decoration into the glaze to give it permanency.

One lady worked on lithography. She cut transfers off sheets of paper and glued them on to pre-glazed pottery, took off the outer transparent film with water then sent them into the kiln to be fired once again. At that point the transfer fused into the glaze.

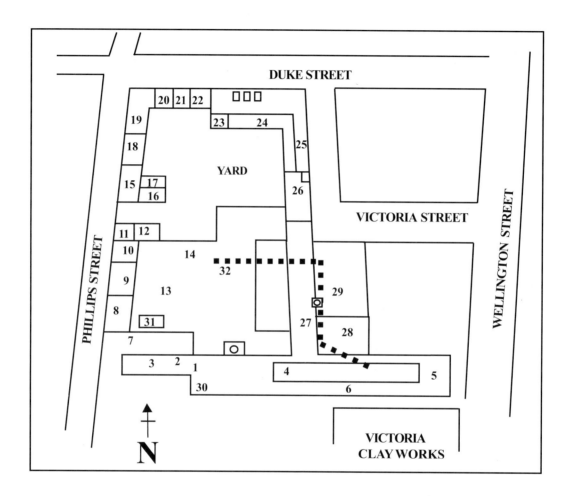

**PHILLIPS POTTERY-1950s**

The map is not to scale. It was compiled from the memories of the pottery work force. It shows the ground floor plan of the working areas at Phillips Pottery around the mid 1950s.

**KEY**

| | | | |
|---|---|---|---|
| 1 | SIEVES | 18 | WAGES OFFICES |
| 2 | BLUNGERS | 19 | CANTEEN AND FOREMAN'S OFFICE |
| 3 | PRESS | 20 | ENTRANCE TO POTTERY, CLOCKING ON/OFF |
| 4 | TUNNEL KILN | 21 | FRANK HARTLEY'S OFFICE |
| 5 | SORTING AREA | 22 | LADIES TOILETS AND BATHING FACILITIES |
| 6 | THROWERS, TURNERS AND SPAYING AREA | 23 | MENS TOILETS |
| 7 | CLAY YARD | 24 | WHITEWARE-CUPS, SAUCERS, DRYING MACHINES |
| 8 | GLAZE STORE (Cliff Haynes) | 25 | WHITEWARE WAREHOUSE |
| 9 | SLIP MIXING SHOP | 26 | WAREHOUSE AND PACKING SHED/ (Henry Ball's Office) |
| 10 | TURNING SHOP | 27 | DRYING PENS AND THROWING AREA |
| 11 | STORE AREA | 28 | DECORATING SHOP |
| 12 | MOULD SHOP | 29 | SECONDS AREA / YARD |
| 13 | STONEWARE DRYING AREA | 30 | DRYING AREA |
| 14 | PRESS HOUSE | 31 | PUG MILL |
| 15 | POTTERY GATE HOUSE | 32 | ROLLER CONVEYOR SYSTEM FROM UPSTAIRS TO KILN AREA |
| 16 | WASH HOUSE | | |
| 17 | TOILETS | | |

Above, a broadside view of the Gibbons Tunnel Oven in 1955 showing the ladies placing wares on the trucks ready to go into the tunnel oven, below three directors of the company Geoffrey Hartley, Lawrence Hartley, Frank Hartley inspecting a truck of pottery ware, newly drawn from the tunnel oven.

The extraction of clay, the use of blungers, sieves, filter presses, pug mills, were part of common processes found at other potteries around the country. Hartleys were part of this common tradition. At their pottery two types of clay were required to manufacture goods. Plastic clay was used for throwing on the wheel and pressing, and liquid slip clay that was poured into moulds. In the 1930s and 1940s the pottery produced domestic wares under the name of 'Hartrox'. This was a guaranteed fireproof brown stoneware used to produce stew pots, jars, bowls, jugs and foot warmers, bottles, bread pots and wash basins. These came in all sizes for kitchen and dairy use and for flower pots. The pottery ware was produced in a variety of ways: thrown, turned, jiggered, jollied, and cast. Over the years new types of machines and methods were tried out and introduced.

## Throwing

*When throwing a pot on a potter's wheel you sit down with what you call a box between your legs. Inside the box there is hot water used for putting on the clay so as to move it into shape and keep it pliable to work. The potter's wheel was made of steel, and it was attached to a rotating shaft that went through the box. The power and speed came from drive belts via a fly wheel that could be controlled by the potter. This was done using a foot pedal.*

*To aid us when making different size jars and pots, we used some primitive guide tools. These were simple sticks made out of willow and marked at different heights. The piece of willow was dropped into the top of the pot to gain a measurement. The correct width of the pot they called the belly.*

*When the clay had left the pug mill, the assistants, often women, would cut off the necessary amount of clay and take it to the thrower. There it was weighed up, for each particular piece of pottery had a specific weight for a size of pot. The clay was beaten, kneaded, to take air out and was then made into a ball. To make a pot which took over five pound in wet clay, the assistant would make two balls of clay, a large one then a smaller ball on top. The first was used to make the bottom of the pot and the other the neck.*

*As a thrower you earned your wage on the piece work rate. For example, in one day your order might be to make twenty dozen six inch Dee Cee jugs and thirty-two dozen pin trays. The pay and task were related to the size of the pot you were making. The sizes ranged from 24s, 18s, 12s, 8s, 6s, 5s, 4s. In the 1950s a dozen 24s bowls paid seven pence. The higher the number of the pot, let's say it was a 4, a large item, the less you had to make to make your wage.*

Thrower Alf Wilson making a large bread bowl at Hartleys in 1955. His assistant Cissie Smith is weighing and knocking up the clay ready for throwing.

*Alf Wilson was a thrower, he used to make big cream pots that went down to Devon. In my eyes he was the champion thrower of the world. I worked at the pottery many years and never saw a thrower as good as him for making the big stuff. He would stand on top of his wheel while someone was treadeling for him. It was that high he couldn't reach it himself.*

Thrower, Wilf Beedle at Hartleys in March 1954 making dog bowls which are then placed on shods. He is being watched by the television presenter Mortimer Wheeler.

A page from the daily note book of Wilf Beedle, a Thrower at Hartleys.

When satisfied the thrower would place the finished item on a plaster-of-paris shod to prevent the pots drying-out too quickly. A series of shods were loaded onto wooden boards. Generally, the boards were left to dry over night. If the weather was warm the pots would dry by themselves but if it was cold the boards were placed on shelves over a series of gas jets to aid the drying process.

Cliff Haynes was the foreman when I was there. He was one of the gentlest men I have ever met in my life. He would go round telling the throwers what the order was for the next day and being generally supportive.

Wilf Beedle was a thrower, he made nothing else but stew pots for ages, for we had a big order to supply a special designed stew pot exclusively to Woolworths.

Our part of the factory was pretty basic in construction, just bare brick walls. It was pretty damp with all the wet clay drying out. I worked up to my arm pits in water and so did every other thrower.

## Turning

I began work at Hartleys in 1946 as a carrier doing odd jobs here and there around the pottery. I did that until I was sent to do my apprenticeship with Charlie Hawthorne, a turner. He was the top man then. When he left I took over his job. My first wage was £1-4s-4d as a boy working the 7am to 8pm shift. The wages were on par with anywhere else in those days. You used to have to negotiate your pay rise with the manager Mr Frank Hartley. Everyone was on different money, with nobody knowing what others were paid. There was never trouble, everyone seemed happy with their pay.

Using a lathe the turner turned a basic pot that had been thrown previously by the thrower, tidied it up, and gave it its final shape. I stood up to work my lathe controlling it with a foot treadle. Mine was an old one, around a hundred years old.

I began the day's work turning the previous day's thrown pottery. These pieces were not fully dried out, grey in colour, with a little dampness in them. This state we *called semi-dry and was the ideal stage to work. The pieces of pottery were stacked in pens on chalk boards. The handler, often a lady, supplied me with my day's work, carrying the heavy fully laden boards to me on her shoulder. The pots were secured to the lathe by pushing them tightly onto a wooden chock, leaving a loose end to work from. This method of working was different and unlike working on an engineering lathe. There the piece of work was fixed at both ends. Different chocks were used for different pieces of pottery, and again for different sizes. I used special tools which I made myself from strips of steel, bent at either end, one with a straight edge and the other shaped to make a footing.*

*I had different tools for turning different pieces of pottery. When turning a pot the first thing that I did was to square off the base of the piece of pottery and put a step on for the foot. I then worked up the pot, before fettling tidying them to take off the rough edges; giving each one a smooth shape. Finally, I polished the pot with a steel polish to give it a lustre.*

*On some of the tall, plain un-decorated stoneware jars and vases we impressed on a circular decorative mark. This was put on the pot while it was on the lathe. A small hand tool had a patterned wheel attached to it. First you dipped the wheel in a dish of paraffin before pressing the wheel on to the revolving vase.*

*I could turn up two to three hundred pieces of pottery a day. I had to keep up with the thrower for what ever he did the previous day I had to be on form to clear them. Some jobs took longer to fettle than the thrower took to throw. After an item had been turned and then dried out it went to be decorated. Some were stippled, with blown glaze others dipped into the glaze.*

## Mould Making

*Just after leaving school I saw the job advertised in the local newspaper. I applied, and started my apprenticeship at Hartleys as a mould-maker. That was in June 1944. I was apprenticed to a Staffordshire man called Bert Bradshaw. He was the head mould-maker at Hartleys for some time. Bert was on the top money, ten pounds* a week, which was a fantastic wage in those days. My apprenticeship lasted seven years. During that time I was called up for my National Service but this was deferred until I had finished my apprenticeship. That meant I was twenty-one years old when I was finally called up. At that time there was only Bert and myself making moulds at the pottery.

Our shop was originally situated upstairs but was later moved to the ground floor. My apprenticeship involved making the different types of moulds and mixing the plaster. The moulds were made from a special pottery plaster which came from Staffordshire. It was quick setting and after twenty minutes it was hard. The master mould was also composed of plaster. Its surface, which would eventually come in to contact with the mixed plaster, had to be first treated with soft soap to prevent sticking. To get the correct texture for the mould the right amount of water and plaster was mixed by hand in a huge jug. The mixing time was crucial. You had to know just when it was the right time to pour the plaster to make the master mould. If you poured too early the water and plaster would begin to separate before the setting process took place. When the mould was set the master mould would be separated and the finished product removed. The process would then be repeated and about four moulds made for each mixing. There were usually about ten dozen per set so this took up quite a lot of time.

If a new product was manufactured it was the responsibility of the head mould-maker to make the first model. If the product had a stated size the shrinkage that occurred during the drying and firing of the clay had to be taken in to consideration to enable the finished product to be the correct size on completion. A drawing would first be produced giving the shape and size, from this the head mould-maker would produce a model using plaster and clay. In the case of a jug the body would be plaster with the spout and handle added in clay. A teapot would have the body and lid in plaster and the spout handle knob for the lid in clay. From this model the first ever mould was produced. A jug would be a three part mould and a tea pot a four part.

Once the original mould was made, master moulds could be made from the original *one and production could begin. In my time I made a variety of moulds used for casting plates, saucers, mugs, and cups. I also made others for use on the jolly machines. We would make moulds in ten dozen batches. We always kept a set of moulds in stock. Our job entailed just making moulds, for they were always breaking and wearing out.*

*A one piece mould was inserted in the jolly machines. Clay was thrown in to the centre of the mould and a profile tool drew the clay up the inside. This formed the outside of the pot. Moulds for plates and saucers were produced the opposite way round. The mould was dome-shaped, and clay was thrown on top of the mould and a profile tool pushed onto the clay. The mould underneath formed the inside of the plate or saucer. Bellying in the upside down position ensured its shape did not warp.*

*Master moulds for handles of cups and mugs were made with a seam down the middle. The mould that made the handles for cups and mugs came in two halves, just like a sandwich cake. Each half of mould had two dozen half handles impressed in to it. When the two halves were placed together the void inside the mould formed a whole handle. The mould was then bound and slip clay was poured in through a hole.*

*I was called up in April 1951, on my return in 1953 Bert had left the company and had been replaced by another Staffordshire mould-maker. I worked there for a while then I moved on to work at Clokie's, eventually becoming the head mould-maker.*

## Jollying and Jiggering

Hollow ware and flatware-making machines were developed in the 1840s and introduced quite widely across the country but only after much resistance a generation later. They are called 'Jollies' because they were thrown by a jollier though where the term originally comes from is unclear. The profile-tool forming the inside shape of a hollow ware item was controlled by the potter but this required less skill or effort than required by a thrower. The outside was shaped by a Plaster-of-Paris mould. The working principle ensured that the plastic clay was shaped with a profile tool pivoted on an arm controlled by the hand of the jollier as the clay revolved. Saucers and plates are referred to as flatware and were made in a similar way except the profile tool or blade made the back of the saucer and not the inside as with the cups. This process was called jiggering.

*In my day the jollier threw a lump of clay in to the centre of the mould. A different mould was used for different pots and different pottery shapes. The clay inside the mould revolved around just like a potter's wheel, the jollier pulling the clay into the revolving mould's sides with his hand and then putting his profile tool in and tooling it around.*

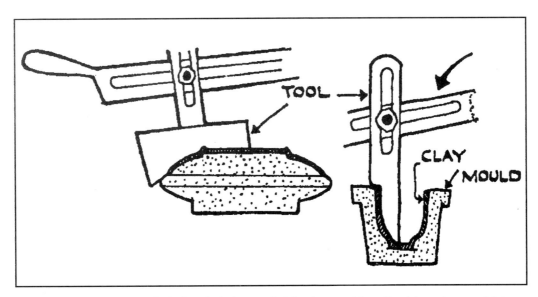

This illustration shows the two methods. Jiggering is shown on the left and was used for making plates and saucers. Jollying, shown on the right, used to make cups and pots.

*Jollier, Henry Hemmingway was one of the quickest men I've seen. As the saying goes he could eat clay. A turtle pot was made in no time at all. He could eat them for breakfast.*

*You didn't specialise, sometimes you had to go on to other jobs, filling in when someone was ill. As a result I had a spell working with the jollier. I had to prepare the clay, cutting lumps off with a wire, weighing it and knocking it up into sizable balls. If you didn't prepare the clay correctly by knocking out all the air when it was placed in the jolly machine it would jump off or break up as it was worked.*

*The jollier worked a retractable handle that incised the ball of clay which had been placed inside a mould that revolved on a turning wheel. The clay was then displaced to fill the mould. This operation took only a few seconds. The plaster-of-Paris mould was then taken out and replaced with another one and the process was repeated over again. I loaded the full moulds on to a board and carried them in to the drying pens. When the piece of pottery inside the mould was semi-dry it was tipped out and the mould was used again.*

*The Whiteware department was on the ground floor. Whiteware meant cups, mugs, and saucers made on jolly machines. The jolly machine which Shirley operated made cups and was automated. It was incorporated into a drying machine, which held four moulds at a time. She would put clay into two of the empty moulds. The machine then lifted them up, spun them round as the profile knives came down into the moulds and made the cup. While this operation was taking place Shirley took the two previously made full moulds off the machine and placed them on an elevator dryer. She replenished the machine with fresh moulds and clay. The full moulds that were drying sat on a tray which went upwards in a revolving motion and came down the other side semi-dried. This operation took around three hours. At the other end of the machine it was the job of two women to take the moulds off the dryer. The cups were then taken out of the moulds and fettled before being placed on a wooden board ready to go to the drying pens. The empty moulds were wiped clean and replaced on the revolving drying shelf. These went down and came back up at the other side where Shirley took them off and placed them back in the jolly machine. She inserted two more blobs of clay, and repeated the process.*

*I worked at Hartleys from leaving school at fifteen until I was called up to do my National Service. My first job at the pottery was upstairs working with the women making milk bottle coolers. I then moved on to work with Ernie Wood. He made oval stew pots and lids on a jolly machine. I carried the empty and full moulds to and fro from the drying pens.*

George Jackson pulling down the arm of the profile tool to make stew pots on a jolly machine, assisted by Betty Pendleton at Hartleys, 1955. Notice that in the background full moulds are placed on a gas fired mangle-type dryer.

*At one point I worked in the whiteware department on the automatic machine that made cups. They placed four cup moulds in the machine. If one didn't produce the cups the other ladies working down the line didn't earn a lot of money. I got paid for doing thirty-six cups to a dozen. Girls kept count on the number of cups I made.*

Marlene Hepworth of Hartleys using the jolly machine to make Coronation ware in 1952.

## Slip Casting

*The slip casting shop was on the first floor and consisted of two separate rooms above the press house. Slip casting was a method of making pottery ware by pouring slip-clay into a plaster mould. The plaster absorbed water from the slip so that a layer of hard clay built up on the inside of the moulds. After a while the surplus slip was poured out of the mould.*

*Cliff Haynes was the foreman in charge. In his casting shop on the ground floor he mixed imported china clay from Cornwall and the pottery's own stoneware clay in a small blunger to make the liquid clay for the slip-casting department. From the blunger the slip was pumped to a holding tank. Cliff measured and weighed a fluid amount of slip to ensure the right consistency for production. The slip was then pumped upstairs to the casting shop.*

*The caster laid out the empty moulds on to large benches ready for the day's production. The mould for a Ure Jug was made of three pieces, two sides and a bottom. These were held together with a rubber band. Each bench had a hose and gun which pumped the slip to fill the moulds. The full mould was inspected frequently to test the thickness of the jug's sides. Once the correct thickness was achieved the moulds were tipped up on their ends to let the excess slip drain out through the bench slats. The surplus slip was drained into a drain tank underneath the bench, then pumped back to the tank and re-used.*

*When the moulds had emptied they were opened up. The jugs were removed to be fettled and sponged down. The jugs were then put on trays and placed in the drying pens over-night. The moulds were later cleaned and refilled. I did all the work on the full moulds for the large Ure Jugs for they were really heavy. The ladies tended to look after all the smaller work like making jardinieres and bowls.*

*Three women made the handles for the cups and mugs. The handles were cast in a large circular plaster mould which was around eighteen inches in diameter. The mould consisted of two halves which fitted together and looked like a sponge*

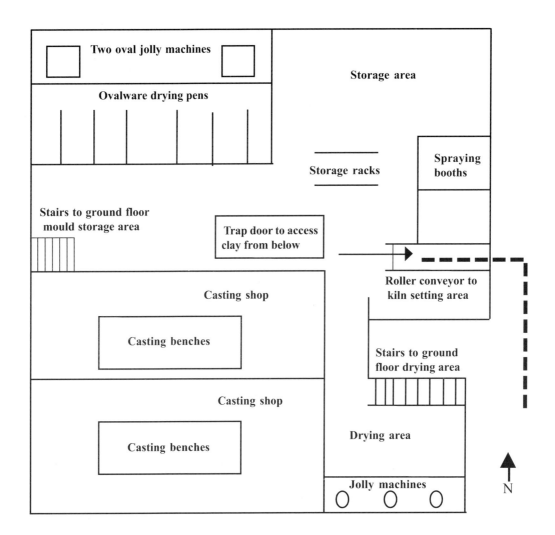

**FIRST FLOOR LAYOUT-PHILLIPS POTTERY-1950s**

The stoneware casting shop. On the benches cast casserole dishes sit on the boards. In the background are the spray booths.

*sandwich. The slip was poured in a hole that ran through the centre of the mould and was then left to set for a while. The mould was split open at the point when the handles were not fully dried out. A small knife was used to release the delicate handles. The handles were then cleaned up and fixed to the cup using liquid slip. The operation ended when the cups were finally tidied up using a small match stick to smooth over intricate places. The cup was then transported to the paint shop to have the transfers stuck on and to be lined with gold prior to glazing and firing.*

*Once the pottery wares had been shaped by throwing, pressing and casting, they were known as green ware. They would often need a little trimming and tidying up to remove all the imperfections. This was called 'fettling'. When the ware was sufficiently dry to handle, the seams and rough edges are sponged and rubbed smooth. The handles and spouts were then added using a little slip.*

Sometimes I put handles on pots for Alf Wilson. He would make around twenty large bread and cream pots a day. I would probably do this for two days a week. You had to work where the work was.

Little was wasted. To the side of the kiln there were great big wicker baskets full of pottery, usually small stoneware posy baskets or little jugs that had tiny cracks where the handles met the pot. When things were a bit slow, and we hadn't much to do in the paint shop, we used to go and sit by the baskets and fill the tiny cracks with plastic wood. This was the exact colour as the fired stoneware pottery

One of the jobs I did at the pottery was making and fixing handles to jugs. To make the handles I had to load clay into a machine that pressed and extruded it through a chuck dye to the required shape. As the clay came out I cut it into long lengths of around four foot and placed them on a wooden board. I then carried the lengths of clay to another department where I cut them to size and fitted them to the semi-dried jugs with liquid slip before shaping.

Joan Dyson at Hartleys in 1955 is making handles for jugs and bottles which are made from extruded clay. Afterwards it was cut into appropriate lengths. In the background are the drying pens which contain fully laden boards of various pieces of pottery.

## Glazing

*I operated a glazing machine that was designed by Mr Stoker. It replaced the old method of internally glazing the pots by pouring the liquid glaze into the pot and swishing it around until it covered the sides. The machine worked on the principle of a fountain. Air pressure pushed the liquid glaze up through a long tube. The required pressure could be regulated by a gauge. I put the pot over the tube, pressed a lever, and whoosh up came the glaze. You had to be careful to ensure you got the correct pressure, for it was easy to get it in your eyes and face. We didn't have any protective masks or glasses in those days. After taking the pot off the machine I wiped down the rim ready for the outside to be sprayed.*

*We applied many different colour glazes. I had to mix my own depending on what the foreman required that day. The plain glaze came in the form of a solid yellow rock. I weighed out two or three pounds of the glaze and put it to steep in a mixing bowl of hot water for two or three hours. This allowed it to soften and break down. To give the liquid glaze a colour Mr Luke, or the foreman, would weigh out and add two or three ounces of a colour additive. It was then left to soak for a while until it was a mushy consistency. Using my hands to squash and stir the glaze I made it in to a smooth texture and then put it through a sieve. The glaze now had the consistency of porridge. It was then watered down and weighed on scales ensuring that the correct amount of water was added to give you the right amount of sheen. After a time you could judge everything to a tee, it was like mixing pudding batter after you'd made it for years.*

*Spray glazing was applied inside an enclosed cabin. The item of pottery was placed on a small revolving turner's wheel and the glaze was applied with an air pressure gun connected to an air pressure hose. The gun was filled up with glaze a cup at a time. The nozzle on the gun could be regulated to give you a variety of spray widths. A large article required more pressure than a smaller one.*

*Usually the glaze was applied in so fine a spray it was like a mist or dust. It covered you all over and when I went home on a night my mum would say, 'You've been spraying green today.' She could tell by the colour of my hair.*

*Spraying was also done at the back of the kiln. This was to give a little more ventilation for the windows which backed on to the clay quarry were sometimes left open over night. This allowed the resident frog population an opportunity to investigate the inside of the pottery. Some mornings when you came into work the large bowls of glaze at the back of the kiln were full of frogs swimming around croaking their heads off. There was loads of them, what a sight.*

*Everybody who sprayed, mixed their own glaze and it took two people to carry this up the stairs to the main spraying room. Downstairs worked The Big Three: Annie, Nellie and Emma. They worked on all the big stuff, the heavy bread bowls. One glazed the inside, the other the outside and the other third carried them away. They were fantastic and worth their weight in gold. They could glaze anything, sprays, dips, everything, they were real workers. Men didn't work as hard as they did.*

*In those days the pottery had no central heating system so it used to be freezing cold in winter. The foreman would come round every half hour or so and let us go and stand in the drying pens to get warm. Sometimes the glazing bays froze over, many times the metal hand spray gun was that cold I had to wrap a rag around it's handle to use it.*

*When part dry Henry Hemmingway used to apply a white coloured watery slip clay into the mixing bowls and swill it around, covering all the insides. When emptied he ran his finger around along the top inside edge of the bowl leaving a plain mark. When the bowl had dried, red lead was applied to the bowl's edge, so when fired, the finished inside of the bowl was white, with a red ring on the inside.*

# THE WORKFORCE

In the early 1950s the pottery employed around about 130 people, half of them women. There were no labour problems for most of the work people lived quite near and others had easy access by public transport. However, attracting juvenile female labour, easy in the pre-war years got harder for they were more attracted by the better wages offered by the local clothing factories. Coal mining, with its high wages, drew off the juvenile male labour. Many of the youths who joined the pottery from school usually returned to the industry after their military service. In those years the pottery built baths so that the work-people could bathe during the mid-day break and after work hours.

The pottery workforce was on the whole stable and committed, one reason being that some workers had other family members working there or had relatives who had worked there before them. This sense of tradition and belonging reflects in their attitude to the pottery.

*The one good thing about the pottery was you enjoyed going to work, it was like one big happy family, there was always a good laugh. The only thing I had against it was that everyone had to individually negotiate their own pay rise and no one told the other person what they had earned. That said all-in-all a good workforce was employed at the pottery. When you were asked to help out on a different job from your own for say half an hour, you were seen alright, being recompensed for your work with the odd teapot or two.*

*My mum was working at the pottery making handles for cups. She heard a job was coming up and put a word in for me. I got the job and for a short while worked as a secretary to the pottery accountant. My work involved typing all his correspondence as well as making the labels for Henry Ball, the warehouse foreman. The address labels were stuck on to the crates and old tea chests packed with straw ready for dispatching out the pottery wares.*

Pottery workers Minnie Wood, Minnie Saunders and Florrie Spears fettling the pieces of pottery

*While at school my friend Norma and I visited the pottery. After our visit the pottery contacted the school asking if anyone of the pupils would like to work there. Norma and I were set on at Hartleys Pottery in 1953. We wanted to get a job in the decorating shop. During our first working day everyone went home due to some breakdown. They left us two new girls on our own with just the foreman to look after us. We were trying our hand at hand decorating the pottery. We had to put brown lines on jugs. Well, we were hopeless, the lines were all over the place. In fact the foreman, being so polite as not to embarrass us, and not to say we had made a mistake, was rubbing off what we had done and repainting the lines on himself.*

*I can always remember our first week's wage. It was £1-19s-11d. They didn't give us two pound notes, but one note and a handful of change, that just for the sake of a penny. As you got older you received a pay rise of half a crown. The women only got half the wage the men got. When I finally finished working there my wage was about £4.*

*We clocked on for work at 8 o'clock in the morning and knocked off at 5 o'clock in the evening We worked a five and a half day a week for we worked Saturday mornings. We didn't have a canteen as such but there was a room with a tea urn in it. You paid for a cuppa and took it back to where you was working. We had one tea break in the morning and an hour for dinner and a break in the afternoon.*

*At dinner time Nellie Varley used to go out for pork pies from a little butchers up the street. We would warm them up for our lunch on the gas jets in the pens. That was the only way we could keep warm, there was no hot food available at the pottery when I worked there.*

*At eighteen years old I worked under Miss Ambler at Hartleys Pottery. She was a strict disciplinarian. She was short and round in stature but none the less she frightened me to death. My job entailed counting the stock, checking the deliveries, packing, ordering of clay, invoicing and paying the wages and on numerous occasions administrating first aid, for I was often called on to take something out of someone's eye or bandage up a finger.*

*One day my old school mistress came on a visit with a party of school girls. At the time I was working with a woman making chamber pots. My old teacher recognised me and said, 'Hello Derek, what are you making?' Feeling rather embarrassed I replied 'Guzunders'. I daren't say chamber pots. Sometimes for a laugh we would make a chamber pot for a birthday or wedding gift, in the bottom of the pot we would paint an eye for a bit of fun.*

*Music was relayed to the pottery by radio from Mercers in Castleford. Each week we had a musical draw out. You gained a tick at the side of your name when your song was played during certain hours in the day. The one with the most ticks by three o'clock on Friday won. I once won with the song Gilly Gilly Ass And Feffa Catsinella Bogum By The Sea. I recall the prize money being thirty shillings, that was a lot of money then, nearly as much as I got as a wage.*

*To keep me warm while working downstairs in the pottery one cold winter someone brought me a metal bucket full of hot ashes and fire. Unfortunately, we soon had to cancel that method of heating for the smoke and ash it gave off was settling all over the pots, and sticking to the glaze.*

*When I came out of the army the pottery had formed a cricket team. Around February time, which is outside the cricket season, I joined the team paying my membership subs of one shilling and sixpence. Shortly afterwards the club disbanded and shared out the pool, I received thirteen pounds back without ever having hit a ball.*

*On a weekend some of the pottery workers went on cycle rides. Myself, Molly, Geoff, and Ginger, along with a few others once went to Skipton. I rode an old sit up and beg bike, the lads had racers. I got as far as Savile Road in Castleford on the way back when I fell off. I wasn't able to get back on so they had to practically carry me home.*

*I lived in Wade's Yard in the Potteries. Many of the people who lived in terrace rows worked at Hartleys pottery. My first job at Hartleys was carrying out, carrying fully laden wooden boards or tins of pottery upon my shoulder. This work was usually done by women. It left a fair ridge impressed into your shoulder. Carrying was the main mode of transporting the pieces of pottery around the factory. It was arduous work stacking boards in the racks in the drying pens, especially when you had to lift them off your shoulder and lift them above your head. I thought to myself, 'I hope I haven't to do this work all the time'. The boss said to me that I had to start at the bottom.*

*Within the pottery there was a roller conveyor belt that carried ware from the upstairs to the downstairs entering the kiln area via a small bob-hole. During my dinner hour as a young lad, around fourteen years old I, with the other lads, played around sitting on trays and roller coasting down the conveyor. One day I came flying down, shot through the bob hole, and bumped straight into Mr Lawrence the pottery owner. He played merry hell with me using a few choice words. He then told me to get sat down, and stop messing around.*

*Albert Mincher was the steam boiler and maintenance man. He and Bill Smart, who we called Scrogg, were often daggers drawn though both of them stood five foot nothing and were built like whippets. You had to laugh at them. You'd go in to the press house only to see them battling like two knights of old duelling with a pair of shovels cursing and carrying on at each other.*

*Sometimes we took visiting parties of people on an informative excursion around the pottery, showing them how it worked. But there was certain parts of the pottery that was out of bounds to the public, for secrets are secrets. A certain amount of espionage went on, so you didn't let everyone know how you did things in case people came and stole your ideas and techniques. You had to keep things close to your chest.*

The pottery yard 1950. Amongst the straw which was used for packing in the crates are Ray Skeates, warehouse worker, Geoffrey Hartley, pottery director, Arthur Carpenter, warehouse worker.

*The imperfect wares we called seconds. These were sold on and bought by hawkers who went round selling our seconds from vans or from a horse and cart. Mr Thompson was a regular. He bought them and sold them from his Castleford shop. Sometimes we put the seconds in the relief yard and smashed them all up. That was good for getting rid of all your frustrations, it was also a lot of fun.*

*Lawrence Hartley was generous to a fault, he knew everyone who worked for him, if any of the works people were ever in trouble he would do what ever he could to help them. After leaving the navy I came back to the pottery. Uncle Lawrence said, 'Go in the fitting shop and get your self a trade', which I did. The fitting shop looked after both works. There we did everything from black smithing to welding, fitting to labouring. The machinery at the pottery and brickworks was very old and parts were often not available so we had to make repair parts ourselves.*

*Many years ago Whitwood Mere was subjected to flooding. The bobby would come around warning us of the expectant flood. When that happened Hartleys who were very good to the people who lived in the nearby houses, ours included, let people go and collect buckets of clay to build little walls in the doorways of their houses, with some bricks kept especially to keep the water out.*

*In the 1950s it was quite easy to get a job in the potteries. You could leave Bradshaws in the morning and walk into a job at Hartleys or Clokie's in the afternoon. Some women used to go around the different potteries, looking for a better job or better pay. If they just got fed up at Bradshaws they would try a spell at Hartleys then move on to Clokie's.*

# NEW WARES

Around 98 % of all the products made at this time were stoneware. The bulk consisted of domestic ovenware, along with dairy-ware such as cream pots, jugs, and milk pans. It was also used for chemical ware. They also produced a large number of bulb bowls, dog bowls, rabbit feeding troughs and nest eggs trays. Later they extended their range and introduced stoneware hot water bottles. These were available with blue, green, purple and yellow glazes.

The demand for the brown stoneware, which was the staple product at Hartleys, did not fluctuate, their orders remained the same from one year to the next. At that time none of the domestic stoneware was exported. A popular and traditional type of product that sold well in Wales and the West Country was the eight gallon pancheon. This was a stoneware bowl used for mixing dough for bread. Another article that sold well was the stew pan, a favourite to customers in Lancashire. Both the pancheon and the stew pan were glazed brown on the outside and clear on the inside.

In February 1952 Hartleys turned their hand to making Coronation Ware to celebrate the coronation of Queen Elizabeth II in July 1953. This type of ware had been recognised for a long time as a favourite product of the neighbouring pottery, Clokie & Co. Initially Hartleys produced two types of beakers and a fruit juice bottle, the latter to be used by firms as a souvenir gift. All three pieces were produced in a shade called Blue Dawn and bore the Royal coat-of-arms. After a while other products such as cups and saucers, bowls, a handled jug, pin trays and preserve jars were added to the Coronation range.

Jean Wilkinson adding a cast handle to a Coronation beaker at Hartleys 1952.

## Art Ware

In 1951/52 Hartleys developed a new range of pottery called Art Ware. This development was probably due to the increasing popularity of other colourful and more modern materials for household use. By this time people were more consumer conscious, they were using more glass and also beginning to switch to plastic containers. These developments impacted on pottery manufacture. The times were also changing, for a market had opened up to the post-war generation, and a variety of colourful modern type of pottery product was now available. Hartleys had to move with the times to be successful and profitable with stiff competition coming from other stoneware manufacturers such as Denby Pottery. To oversee this new venture the works brought in to head a new department a former studio potter L. P. Luke. He combined three roles of artist, ceramicist and chemist.

*Mr Luke came to Hartleys in 1952. He had been a headmaster at a school near York and had dabbled in making glazes for pottery. Hartleys was the only pottery around at the time to fire glazes at a high temperature to create the colours, and this interested him.*

*Up to his arrival there was no art decorating of pottery at Hartleys so to set up the decorative side of the business he put an advert in the local press saying that he required painters. I applied and was set on. I was one of the first to begin decorating. My friend Doreen came along soon after.*

*Some of us decorators had been in art colleges where decorating pottery was part of the course. I was studying dress design and construction but it was very difficult to get a job in that line then so I went to Hartleys to get work. At that time there was no proper paint shop so we were placed in a small area next to the churner in the clay preparation area to work. The initial colour ware was basically just colour slips. The paints we applied looked nothing like the colour until they came out of the kiln fired.*

*I began work at Hartleys Pottery in 1952 as a young seventeen year old girl. I didn't live far from the pottery. A friend of mine worked there, hand painting and gilding cups and plates, she helped me get a job there.*

*Initially I worked in the decorating shop applying transfers on to commemorative ware, cups, saucers and plates which were in production for the forthcoming Coronation of Queen Elizabeth II. The working hours were from 8.30am until 4.40 pm, with a dinner break. I went home for dinner for the pottery was just across the street. The working surroundings in those days were basic but clean. We had just white washed brick walls and a pot bellied stove to keep us warm. I enjoyed doing the transferring work.*

*Later I was offered a job hand painting. I grasped at the chance. We had to work quite fast but earned some good bonuses. Mr Luke was our immediate boss and Mr Geoffrey Hartley was the boss of the overall decorative side of the operation. The decorative patterns were designed by Mr Luke and some of the other girls had attended Art College. Mr Luke was also responsible for mixing the colours of the paint and glazes.*

*Sat at my bench I would begin decorating a piece of pottery by picking it up from the board, putting my hand inside the piece and placing it on to the wheel that revolved. It was essential to centre the item. This I did by spinning and knocking the item. First I put the fine lines of paint on each piece then put them to one side before repeating the process again, putting on the different width lines. The line work was done first before you put on the final design. I had a number of different pots of paint. We applied the paint with beautiful high quality brushes made from squirrel hair, ideal for they held lots of paint. The paint used was water based and had the consistency of poster paint. It dried really quickly when on the pottery.*

*When decorated, the piece was marked with your initial. The Pottery's manufacturing trade mark was sometimes hand written, but mainly we used a rubber stamp for the Hartrox mark. It is not rare to put on information numbers which related to design codes. The decorated item was then placed on another board.*

A broad view of the decorating shop in 1955. Brenda Pearson, Wyn Lewis, Joan Richards, John Lindley, Anne Dunn, June Pugh, Doreen Hartley and Anne Robinson. They are hand painting under-glaze decorations.

*It was a pleasure to go to work. Something I remember distinctly, in the paint shop for instance, on the bare wall was an old calendar of a Red Indian in full head dress. We were all fond of the old thing so we never ever changed it for a new one. We also had a pot bellied stove fire which had a steel flue. It was also good for warming up pies at dinner time.*

*To come up with new designs to decorate the pottery Mr Luke and a few others in the department would get their heads together and band a few ideas around. Then they were into a period of trial and error. This took place until the bosses said 'Yes that will sell'. From then on that design was patented and put into production. The Peasant Ware, for example, was a very popular and successful range, for you could add a wide range of decorated pieces such as domestic jugs, vases, and bowls. As the time passed we tried other techniques. Mr Luke was responsible for bringing in the air gun technique for glazing. This was done in an enclosed type cabin where the item of pottery was put on to a small wheel and spun around and glazed. The exhaust fumes created were extracted by a fan.*

Art ware decorators, Wyn Lewis, Anne Robinson, June Pugh in the mid 1950s.

*I started work at Hartleys in 1953 and was glad to be back in the pottery business because that is what I enjoyed doing best. At that time the pottery was producing commemorative Coronation items by applying transfers onto the whiteware of cups, saucers and plates. I was acquainted with this work for I used to work at the nearby Clokie Pottery. However, Hartleys were experiencing difficulties. After all their efforts, they had not mastered the art of applying gold lining to the ware. I found myself taking over that process and supervising the firing.*

*Putting gold gilding on the pottery wares was done by hand. The gold came in a tiny bottle. When wiping off the excess gold from the piece of pottery, the cloth used had to be saved and sealed in a container and sent back to the company that supplied it. There the gold was extracted from the cloth to be reused. The gold when applied to the pottery was dark brown in colour. It was only when it had been fired that you got the true colour of gold.*

In 1955 the pottery employed ten decorators. This was a period of innovation. One, a former pupil of Leeds School of Art was Miss Anne Robinson. Along with modelling items she was also capable of mould making, design and hand painting.

The prospect for increased trade in the Art Ware was much greater at that time and so that side of the business was developed. After much experimentation Hartleys succeeded in developing an attractive range of high temperature colours. Existing lines such as jugs, bowls, vases, cup and saucers, tea pots, casserole dishes, lamp stands, were decorated as well as new and tried novelties for the horticultural, catering and filling trades. Items like pin-trays, wall pockets, jardinieres, sabots and swans posy baskets, log troughs, boats and posy rings to hold flowers, came into production and were decorated, stapled or colour glazed in the pottery. Most were decorated to suit traditional tastes, others were 'contemporary' in their appeal.

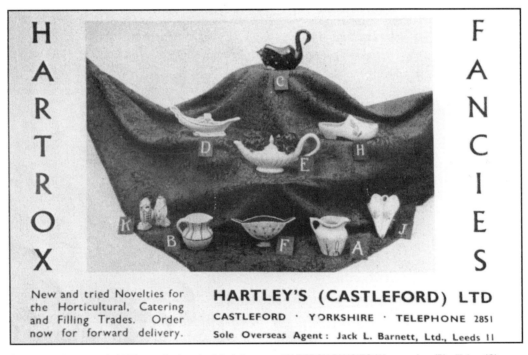

HARTROX FANCIES

New and tried Novelties for the Horticultural, Catering and Filling Trades. Order now for forward delivery.

**HARTLEY'S (CASTLEFORD) LTD**
CASTLEFORD · YORKSHIRE · TELEPHONE 2851
Sole Overseas Agent: Jack L. Barnett, Ltd., Leeds 11

On show at the pottery in 1955, genuine hand painted stoneware HARTROX FANCIES (A) cream jug, (B) milk jug, (C) swan, (D) gondola, (E) Sabot, (F) jardiniere, (J) wall pocket, (H) clog, ( K) condiment set.

In addition to their ornamental lines Hartleys introduced a set of hand painted tiles with twelve different nursery characters for the use as tea pot stands or kitchen decoration. The tiles were colourful and distinctive. Designed by Audrey Limbert, the tiles measured four and a half inches square and could be purchased framed or unframed in any design with special requirements to order.

*In 1955 times were getting hard in the pottery industry, we were always on the look out for new techniques and new ideas. One of the things we had a go at was hand decorating small tiles. We didn't manufacture the tiles, they were brought in for me to decorate from a company called Boots. I designed and illustrated a series of tiles on the theme of nursery rhymes. We also did some kitchen tiles decorated with fruit and other kitchen items. In those days it was uncommon to have the luxury of decorated tiles, let alone hand decorated ones.*

During the mid 1950s Hartleys experimented with hand decorated products they called 'after-use containers'. They were stoneware bottles and jars for supplying food and drink to manufacturers. The idea being that the containers would encourage the sale of the contents but also be useful as an attractive ornament or container after use. The pottery also made a small amount of earthenware products at this time, mainly mugs, beakers, chamber pots and odd cups decorated or plain.

Hartleys distributed their products widely throughout the UK and the Channel Islands, with family member and director Arthur Rhodes travelling around the country gaining orders. They also employed five other representatives who covered the whole of the UK. In addition to this they exported stoneware goods to far away countries such as New Zealand, Australia and Fiji. Mr Jack Barnett was the company's sole exporter agent.

To move with the times Hartleys made headway to expand its products range and its distribution. In the *Pottery Gazette and Glass Trade Review* (April 1955) Frank Hartley described the current market for stoneware products:

*Generally speaking, pottery buyers of today tend to be given less freedom for initiative than their predecessors in the years between the wars. Whereas a buyer was formerly allowed to buy what he knew or thought he could sell easily he is today more subject to control of spending by a merchandise manager, and frequently by the directors. There was a regrettable tendency to avoid offering the public the rather more bulky items such as the typical brown and clear glazed products of stoneware producers. In London particularly it was rather difficult to get the stockists to give prominence to displays of 3 and 4 pint casseroles and similar items, as they were more inclined to do with competitive heat resisting glassware. Though these were not always lower priced than the stoneware.*

*The lack of interest in stoneware of that description could probably be attributed to the lack of storage space. There is a demand there, and it should be encouraged by stockists. The prospects in the stoneware industry were brighter now than they had been for many years. People are beginning to realise that for cooking there was nothing quite so good.*

Although the pit falls of the stoneware industry were highlighted by Mr Hartley he was optimistic about the pottery's future, for Hartleys had added beauty to their stoneware, especially in the hand decorated floral on-glaze decorations. In 1957 Hartleys (Castleford) Ltd. Phillips Pottery, advertised themselves on their letter heads as makers of HARTROX FIREPROOF STONEWARE, EARTHENWARE, HARTLEY'S FAMOUS HAND PAINTED HORTICULTURAL WARE and PEASANT POTTERY.

At this time the company was still run as a family concern with H. Lawrence Hartley JP (Managing Director), and John William Hartley, Frank L. Hartley, Charles A. Hartley, Arthur H. Rhodes, and Geoffrey S. Hartley the other company directors. The company seemed to be thriving but it was given a body blow with the death in 1956 of Lawrence Hartley, its prime mover. At this point Frank Lawrence Hartley took over running the pottery. Three years later in March 1959 Hartleys, progressive as ever, introduced a new line of pottery, *Yorkshire Oven and Tableware*. It was an instant success and was exported to Australia, and in demand nearer to home in the shops of Leeds, Bradford and other Yorkshire cities as well as Manchester, all stocked the new product. The works manager at that time was P. R. Channell, formerly of Royal Doulton. In an extract from the *Pontefract and Castleford Express* he stated:

*The whole thing started last August as a vague idea when an Australian firm talked of black and pink pottery. The germ of an idea grew slowly, new processes designs, materials and colours were discussed and about a month ago the first pieces went into production with highly satisfactory results.*

The new products were made from a finer clay imported from Devon. The range consisted of an oval pie dish and an oval casserole in three sizes, a round casserole in four sizes, a dual purpose casserole, saucepan, cereal bowl in two sizes, beaker and nursery beaker, plates in three sizes, roaster and gravy boat. They were produced with black and pink interiors, or with grey in place of the black and combined with plumb, turquoise, pale blue or sunshine yellow. The prices at the time were one shilling and four pence for the nursery beaker, to twelve shillings and seven pence for the large casserole. Along side these new wares the traditional stew pots, bread crocks, pudding basins and flower vases and the blue and white striped kitchen items were still being made. As were mustard pots and marmalade jars.

A selection of the Yorkshire Oven and Tableware that was introduced in 1959.

The new *Yorkshire Oven and Tableware* range added to the existing Horticultural Ware, Hartrox Fireproof Stoneware and the Earthenware. The company were also contractors to the Admiralty and War Office. Despite this the pottery seemed to be in trouble, maybe due to lack of orders through low consumer demand for stoneware products, or financial difficulties. It was recognised that there was a need to down scale the operation and eventually the pottery's workforce of one hundred and twenty people were given their terminating notice in June 1959. The pottery closed in the autumn of that year.

*After the closure I went to work at Pollards in Ferrybridge. Six months later I received a letter from Hartleys asking if I would like to go back to work at the pottery, a new manager interviewed me. He asked me if I preferred pottery work to engineering, I replied, 'Pottery of course'. After some negotiation he asked if I would come back to work for five shillings and three halfpennies an hour. I said 'I would'. It was the same money.*

Hartleys were down but not out, after six months Phillips Pottery took on a number of ex-employees and reopened after undertaking a refit and modernisation. They replaced the tunnel kiln with two smaller electric kilns. These held only four trucks.

With the staff reduced to forty people the Phillips Pottery celebrated the New Year with production restarting on January 1st 1960. The company had acquired orders and contracts. It continued its export trade and the home market seemed satisfactory. With high hopes the pottery anticipated to be in full swing in the middle of February with the new line in pottery to be exhibited in Blackpool Show in the March.

However, all hopes and expectations of a second chance to pull the pottery side of the company around did not materialise. In October, only ten months after it reopened, manufacturing came to a halt and the pottery closed yet again. The managing director Frank Hartley summed up the difficulties at the time, stating:

*'There has been competition from plastics and glassware. The pottery used to make Brown Ware but people want more decorative pottery these days. The firm could not*

*get sufficient skilled labour to make it and we were unable to sell at competitive prices. The question of price would have been settled if the labour had been available and efforts to meet the new demands, and to obtain export trade, had met with success. The labour situation however appears to have been decisive. Skilled workers were not available locally.*

The loyal workforce, which was once again out of work, recall those final days as the oldest pottery in the Castleford district finally ended production.

*Unfortunately the new production ways at the pottery didn't work out as planned for there were too many teething troubles. It never got in to full production and closed after six months. I was one of the last to leave.*

*There were no conciliation discussions on closure. All we saw was a notice which went up on the board near the kiln, close to where the factory clock was situated. I asked Betty, the girl who I was working with, to check the time. On her return she said 'Bloody hell, have you seen that notice in there. We're closing in a fortnight'.*

*When the pottery closed all we got was a glass of port and a 'sorry we are closing'. I went for a job interview at the nearby pottery of Clokie's. I turned their offer down after he told me what the job entailed and the pay. The Clokie's manager asked me what I earned at Hartleys. I replied 'Five shillings and three half pennies an hour'.*
*He replied, 'No wonder they've closed down!'*

ESTABLISHED UPWARDS OF A CENTURY

DIRECTORS :
FRANK L. HARTLEY
JOHN WM. HARTLEY
GRACE HARTLEY

"HARTROX"
FIREPROOF
STONEWARE
———

EARTHENWARE

YOUR REF.

OUR REF.

# Hartleys (Castleford) Ltd.
## Phillips Pottery
### Castleford
#### Yorkshire

TELEPHONE No. 2851-2
TELEGRAMS :
" PHILLIPS POTTERY, CASTLEFORD "
———
CONTRACTORS TO
ADMIRALTY AND WAR OFFICE
———

HARTLEYS
YORKSHIRE OVENWARE
HORTICULTURAL WARE

9th June, 1959

R. Skeates Esq.,

Dear Mr. Skeates,

     You will have observed the notice that has been posted regarding the close-down of this factory and it is with regret therefore that we must give you notice terminating your employment with us on the 23rd June, 1959.

     We should like to extend our thanks for your past services.

Yours faithfully,
HARTLEYS (CASTLEFORD) LTD.

# THE WARES

A selection of the typical pre-Second World War pottery wares made at Phillips Pottery. Left, red earthenware bread mixing bowl unglazed on the outside with a cream glaze on the inside, not marked. Centre, unmarked stoneware preserve jar with a brown glaze to the neck. Right, large red earthenware bread pot, clear glaze on the inside, brown glaze to half way down on the outside, not marked. Front, a stoneware oval dish impressed Phillips Castleford.

Top, Selection of HARTROX stoneware pottery. Back, spill vase 24cm high x 17cm wide, vase 26cm high x 20cm wide. Centre left, bulb bowl 19cm high x 11cm wide, bowl 10cm high x 20cm wide, vase 15cm high x 15cm wide. Front, beaker 10cm high x 7cm wide.

They are all plain and un-glazed on the outside being buff in colour, and have only a clear glaze on the inside. All are stamped marked HARTROX-STONEWARE-CASTLEFORD and have an additional stamp WRCC (West Riding County Council) which were made and used for the local schools.

Left, a traditional stew pot was a staple product finished with a rich brown glaze, 16cm high x 19cm wide impressed on the lid HARTROX.

Hartleys Coronation ware. Above left, glazed in a light green colour a stoneware bulb bowl 20cm high x 11cm wide stamped HARTROX STONEWARE CASTLEFORD. Right, a handled jug 12cm high x 10cm wide coloured in dawn blue, stamped HARTROX ENGLAND. Left, stoneware preserve jar 10cm high x 9.5cm wide coloured in blue dawn glaze and stamped HARTROX STONEWARE CASTLEFORD.

Top, hand decorated pin trays with applied Coronation transfers 12cm wide x 2.5cm high, not marked.

Bottom, tea cup, saucer and beaker, with gold band. These items were commonly referred to as White ware.

Top, a photograph shows pieces from the firm's range of hand painted ornamental and useful artware from 1955. (A) Juno jug, (B) Pandora vase, (C and D) nut and fruit bowls, (E) butter dish, (F) Chinese bowl, (G) crocus bowl, (H) polyanthus bowl, (J) spill vase, (K) un-handled beaker, (L) Pinder jug (M) handled beaker and (O) bottle jug.

Right, floral decorated vase, 20cm high x 16cm wide, hand marked Hartrox, Individual Pottery.

Far right, decorated vase, 26cm high x 16cm wide, hand marked HARTROX, Individual Pottery.

A selection of stoneware items hand decorated Art ware . Back left, jug decorated in the Peasant range 27cm high x 12cm wide, stamped marked HARTROX STONEWARE CASTLEFORD, back right, a Pandora vase 24cm high x 15cm wide, hand marked HARTROX. Front left , jug 18cm high x 12cm wide, hand marked DEE CEE, front right, Juno jug 15cm high x 12cm wide, hand marked HARTROX.

Hand decorated Art Ware. Left, blue vase, 27cm high x 16cm wide, impressed MADE IN ENGLAND and hand marked Individual Pottery, Hartrox. Right, vase 20cm high x 14.5cm wide, hand marked Individual Pottery, Hartrox.

Examples of two tea sets hand decorated in Art Ware. Top back left, teapot 11cm high x 11cm wide , centre, teapot 12cm high x 13cm wide, fruit dish 5.5cm high x 22cm wide, centre left, marmalade pot 10cm high x 10cm wide, milk jug 8cm high x 9cm wide, tea pot 11cm high x 11cm wide, front sugar bowl 4cm high x 9 cm wide, marmalade pot 10cm high x 10cm wide. All the items are stamped Dee Cee ENGLAND.

Bottom left, teapot 13cm wide x 11cm high, stamped HARTROX-STONEWARE-CASTLEFORD and hand marked Individual Pottery. Milk jug 9cm wide x 8cm high stamped HARTROX-STONEWARE-CASTLEFORD, and hand marked Individual pottery.

A selection of stoneware hand decorated Art Ware items. Left, jug 21cm high x 16cm wide stamped marked Dee Cee ENGLAND and hand marked Individual pottery. Top right, jug 17cm high x 13cm wide, hand marked Hartrox, bowl 9cm high x 23.5cm wide hand marked Hartrox. Bottom right, jug 21.5cm high x 16cm wide hand marked Dee Cee.

Top, selection of Yorkshire Ovenware, back, pink circular dinner plate 22cm wide x 22cm high, blue oval dinner plate 29.5cm wide x 2cm high, centre, blue casserole dish 26cm wide x 5cm high, yellow casserole dish 31cm wide x 5cm high, front, pink casserole dish 20.5cm wide x 4.5cm high, all marked HARTLEYS (Castleford) Ltd Yorkshire Ovenware. Left, Casserole dish and lid glazed in sunshine yellow 24cm wide x 12cm high marked HARTLEYS (Castleford) Ltd Yorkshire Ovenware.

A selection of items made by the slip casting method. Top, kitchen jug 12cm high x 9cm wide stamped DEE CEE Stoneware ENGLAND, large bowl 9cm high x 18cm wide impressed DEE CEE STONEWARE, small bowl 6cm high x 11cm wide marked HARTROX STONEWARE CASTLEFORD, jug 12cm high x 8cm wide marked HARTROX STONEWARE CASTLEFORD. They have been decorated with stippled brown glaze effect.

Left, floral decorated jardiniere 12cm high x 32cm wide marked Dee Cee ENGLAND.

# MANUFACTURING MARKS

Stamp mark, found on a variety of stoneware products with references to hand painted dishes, floral jugs, spill vase, and the horticultural fancies such as logs, boats, bulb troughs, bowls, clogs.

Stamp mark, found on a variety of stoneware products with references to jugs, spill vase, bowls, dog bowl, hand painted tea pots.

Stamp mark, found on a variety of stoneware products with references to hand painted floral jugs, crocus and polyanthus bowls, milk jug. Colour glazed wall pocket, bulb bowls, jugs, pin tray, polyanthus bowl, log trough. Transferred printed bowls, Coronation ware bulb bowls and preserve jars.

Stamp mark, found only on the Oven and Tableware range introduced in 1959. References to oval pie dish, casserole dish, saucepan, cereal bowl, soup cup and saucer, beaker, dinner plate, roaster.

Stamp mark, found on a variety of stoneware products with references to white glazed mixing bowls, combed effect bulb bowls.

Impressed mark, reference to brown glazed stew pot.

Impressed mark, reference to small cream jug.

Stamp mark, 'Vitrified' in blue, reference to on-glaze transfer whiteware commemorative tyke mug.

Impressed mark, reference to whiteware drinking beaker.

Stamp mark, found on a variety of stoneware products with references to un-decorated bowls, spill vase. Hand decorated jugs, crocus bowl. Coloured glazed horticultural fancies such as jardiniere, bulb troughs, posy ring, jugs, bulb log, boat. Blue Coronation vase. Large drinking water storage jar. Mixing bowl.

Impressed mark, found on terra cotta plant pots.

Hand written mark, found on a variety of stoneware products reference to hand painted floral vases, crocus and polyanthus bowls, floral jug, and fruit dishes. Horticultural fancies on swans, beaker, clogs, bowls. Commemorative bottle jug and perfume bottle. In some cases it also accompanies the hand written mark Individual Pottery.

Hand written mark, Individual Pottery is found on hand decorated wares that are unique in that the decorative design is not repeated. References to floral vase, floral jugs, fruit dish, tea pot, milk jug, It can appear on its own, or in some cases it accompanies stamped and hand written Hartrox marks and Dee Cee.

Impressed mark, reference stoneware oval casserole dish

Impressed mark, found on a variety of stoneware products reference to coloured glazed kitchen jug.

Impressed mark, found on stoneware stew pots. An underlined number denotes the various sized pot. Reference to pot sizes 8, 18, 24, 30, 36.

Impressed mark, reference to stoneware mixing bowls that holds 3 and 5 pints.

Stamp mark, reference to stoneware bulb trough.

A familiar mark that can be found stamped, impressed, or hand written appears on many pieces of Hartleys pottery products from the 1950s, is that of Dee Cee. These are the initials for Desmond Cooper. He was a prolific buyer of Hartrox pottery. He visited the pottery and asked for his own lines of produce to be decorated to meet the small gift market which were purchased at the seaside resorts. The Dee Cee marks found on the many plain stoneware products and the more attractive Art ware can be attributed to Hartleys for they are the self and same pieces in form and decoration, and in some cases bare the identification marks of the pottery decorator. However, you have to be aware that Desmond Cooper travelled to other potteries and had items made there. He stamped his marks on their wares too.

# DECORATOR'S MARKS

Doreen Hartley

Terry Durham

Ann Dunn

Ethel Varley

June Pugh

Eileen Sparling

Ann King

Wyn Lewis

John Lindley

Robert Vallance

CW

Colin Weatherall

# BRICK MANUFACTURING

Impressed  HARTLEY

Impressed  HARTLEYS CASTLEFORD Ltd.

Impressed  HARTLEY & Co. CASTLEFORD

Impressed  J H (JOSHUA HARTLEY)

Impressed  HARTLEYS CASTLEFORD

Impressed  J HARTLEY & C CASTLEFORD

Impressed  H CASTLEFORD

# CASTLEFORD BRICKWORKS AND POTTERIES

**1848**
Bateson & Brothers
Fletcher Isaac
Powell Thomas
Sykes William

**1857**
Taylor & Hartley
Winterbottom Jas
Phillips James
Smithson Wm
Wilson Thomas

**1875**
Sykes & Macvay & Co.
McDowall Robert
Phillips Charles
Breffit Edgar & Co.
Hartley Joshua
Taylor & Hartley

**1888**
Clegg John & Thomas
Sykes Mcvay & Co
Hartley Joshua
Phillips C & Son

**1904**
Castleford Brick Co Ltd
Clegg Thomas & John
Hartley Joshua & Co
Healdfield Brick Co
Ridge Field Brickworks Co Ltd
Hattan Charles

**1932**
Hartleys (Castleford) Ltd
Chas Hattan Ltd
Yorkshire Brick Co Ltd

List of Castleford Brickworks and Potteries from local trade directories.

**1822**
Fletcher I (black)
Russell T.S (stone)

**1848**
Bateson & Brothers
Fletcher Isaac
Taylor & Harrison
Wood & Nicholson

**1857**
Clegg John and Thomas
Dickinson Thomas (stoneware)
Harling & Phillips (stone & black)
Hurdus & Asquith
Lowther & Ford
McDowall Hugh & Co. Eagle Pottery
Nicholson Thomas & Co.
Taylor & Harrison
Taylor & Hartley
Wilson James

**1866**
Bateson Thomas & William
Gill George, Providence Pottery
Harling Jas & Son
Lowther & Ford, Calder Pottery
Nicholson T. & Co., Castleford Pottery
Phillips Charles, Mere Pottery
Roberts Jno & Co.
Taylor & Harrison

**1886**
Bateson Thomas & William
Gill George, Providence Pottery
Harling Jas & Son
Lowther & Ford, Calder Pottery
Nicholson T & Co., Castleford Pottery
Phillips Charles, Mere Pottery
Roberts Jno & Co.
Taylor & Harrison

**1892**
Clokie & Co., Castleford Potteries
Ford Brothers, Victoria Pottery
Gill Wm & Sons, Providence Pottery
Harling & Son, Whitwood Mere
Phillips C. & Son, Whitwood Mere
Robinson Brothers, Eleven Acres Pottery

**1927**
Bradshaw Hy & Son, Methley Rd
Clokie & Co., Pottery St
Gill Wm & Son, Leeds Rd
Phillips C & Co., Methley Rd
Robinson Harry, Nicholson St

**1950**
Bradshaw Hy & Son Ltd, Methley Rd
Clokie & Co., Pottery St
Hartley (Castleford) Ltd, Phillips Pottery

# BIBLIOGRAPHY

Diana Edwards-Roussel *The Castleford Pottery 1790-1821* (1982)

Heather Lawrence *Yorkshire Pots and Potteries* (1974)

Dianne Baker *Potworks The Industrial Architecture of the Staffordshire Potteries* (1991)

Jack Dadd and Alan Rogers *Exploring Pottery* (1967)

David Sekers *The Potteries* (1994)

West Yorkshire Archaeology Service *Roman Castleford - Three Volumes* (1998-2000)

WMDC, Art Galleries and Museums *Common Clay* (1987)

Martin Hammond *Bricks and Brickmaking* (1990)

West Yorkshire Metropolitan County Council *In Search of Roman Castleford* (1984)

# PHOTOGRAPHS AND ILLUSTRATIONS

Hartnup & Jarvis, p8. John Goodchild Collection, p15, p17. Ordnance Survey, p 18, p 21, p 22, p45. Pat Bentley, p25.Castleford Handbook 1965, p25. Ron Rockett, p25. David Wilson, p28. Private, p35, p46, p52, p67. Wakefield Metropolitan District Council Libraries & Information Services, p53. Tableware International, p55, p58, p60, p69, p73, p74, p88, p90, p91, p92, p103. Pontefract & Castleford Express, p70, p85, p95. Wilf Beedle, p61, p62. Wyn Winstanley, p89. Ray Skeates, p82, p98. Peter Spears p78. Wakefield Museum and Arts p26. David G. Wilders, p13, p30, p31, p33, p34, p36, p39, p42, p56, p72, p99, p100, p101, p102, p103, p104, p105, p106, p107, p108, p109, p110, p111, p112, p113, p114, p115, p116, p117.